Think On These Things

Think On These Things

90 ENCOURAGING MEDITATIONS FOR SPIRITUAL GROWTH

DR. GEORGIA POINTER

3 TREES

Think on These Things

ISBN: 979-8-9854130-2-1

LCCN: 2023923027

For information contact: ordinerrygirl@yahoo.com

3Trees Publications

18024 Dedeaux Clan Road Gulfport, MS 39574

3 TREES
PUBLISHING

Acknowledgments

I wish to thank the precious prayer warriors in the Debbie Day Class for their faithful prayers for me as I worked to finish this book. I felt those prayers and praise God for each of you. Thank you to Charlana Kelly for your continued service to me in this still new-to-me world of book-writing. You are an answer to my heart's groanings too deep for words. I am thankful the Father heard them and sent you to me.

To Angela at 3Tress Publishing, we have yet to meet face to face, but our hearts are knit together by Christ, and I am blessed that God handpicked you for this exciting leg of my journey in obedience. To Paula, thank you for your generous spirit and beautiful photography. May the Lord open many doors to you.

Thank you to Sandy Morris, who rekindled a dream I thought had died with just five words you probably don't recall saying: "Georgia, you should be writing!"

Finally, to Laura Rivera, whose servant's heart is heard in every phone encounter, thank you for your expertise in creating the book cover.

Introduction

It has been God's plan all along that your life bear much fruit, my friend. The more you grow and the longer you grow, the richer and sweeter the fruit will be. You will be thrilled when you finally see Him face to face, and you must turn sideways to look at Him because of the abundance you will be carrying to throw at His feet. I picture Jesus looking at you with a loving grin because of what you and He produced together. This book is like a seed catalog brimming with many ways Jesus wants to grow you. May every seed fall in fertile soil in your heart and reap a bountiful garden of Christlikeness.

Whatever Is True

DAY 1
IT IS TIME TO STOP YAWNING

Hebrews 11

Adventure. Don't you crave it?

Is it possible to have real adventure as a follower of Jesus Christ? Or is it all just quiet prayers, submissive service, and meek conformity to a dull idea of biblical womanhood?

Adventure happens when you encounter something you did not expect...where the outcome is uncertain, and a task calls upon every ounce of strength you can muster...where the stakes are high, but the reward is even higher. Can a Christian woman experience such a life without violating her femininity and love for God? Absolutely!

In fact, I dare say that if your walk with Christ makes you yawn, it's not His fault. The saints in Hebrews 11 experienced joy, heartache, and amazing miracles, but no one would describe their life as a yawn. By faith, they obeyed God and lived a life of fantastic adventure. What might you be missing because of fear, insecurity, or outright disobedience?

God calls every believer to a life of adventure. What other protagonist has the devil himself as her nemesis? Is there any other heroine who has the superpowers of the Holy Spirit for doing great exploits? What other life of adventure can be more exciting than rescuing real people from a literal hell?

What heart would not beat wildly at doing something she was afraid to do but didn't dare not do for the love of Someone Else?

Dear Sister, the Christian life is a swashbuckling, mind-blowing, lionhearted life. Are you not living it?

If not, may I suggest you tear up that dog-eared list of excuses you gave God last time He told you to do something that scared you to death?

Stop the yawning and step up, my friend. Your adventure with Him awaits!

Think On This

God loves you
too much
to let your identity
be grounded in
what you do.
He tethered
your identity to Something
changeless
so that
you can be secure forever.

(Jeremiah 33:3)

3

Think On This

It may be easy

to shoot the messenger,
but the truth she tells

cannot die.

Whatever is Noble

DAY 2
REDEEM THE TIME

Be very careful, then, how you live—not as
unwise but as wise, making the most of every
opportunity, because the days are evil.

— EPHESIANS 5:15-16

What are you waiting for, my friend? God has given you a dream that He intends you to fulfill. Does fear keep you from moving forward? How long will you pray without action?

People need what God has given you, so do not deprive them any longer.

God has an answer for every excuse you make, but you will not know them unless you get moving. You will remain stuck if you wait until you have all the answers. Start small if you must but start! Do what you can with what you have until God provides more. Take the bold step of letting a safe person know about your dream. This can be powerful because you need accountability.

I watched a movie about a soldier who had psychosis. He saw people that weren't there. They followed him everywhere. When he got better, he was asked if he still saw people who were not there, and he said he did. He just learned not to let those phantoms stop him. The same is true with fear. It may never leave; you must learn not to let it stop you.

Sometimes, being overwhelmed hinders us. The solution is to pick one thing within your power to do today and do it. It is incredible how clear the next step becomes after that.

The momentum God brings will be exciting, and you will wonder why you waited so long.

When you view your dream as something optional, you will lag. You will take your dream more seriously when you see it as a divine assignment with lives on the line. Think on these things.

Whatever Is Right

DAY 3

BEWARE!

*Do not conform to the pattern of this world, but
be transformed by the renewing of your
mind.*

— ROMANS 12:2

We may feel internal or external pressure to conform to the world's way of handling problems. On the surface, the world's solutions may seem logical, but a closer look reveals a form of self-sufficiency that leaves God out. There is nothing new under the sun; the devil repackages the same false solutions to deceive people into depending on anything other than the God Who made them and loves them.

Unsuspecting Christians who buy into those remedies always make things worse.

Unbelievers tag biblical solutions as fanatical, irrelevant, or, at worst, merely religious. This is to be expected since they don't know God as we do, but the Christians who have experienced intimacy with God know better. Who better to fix a product than the original manufacturer? Why would God send His only Son to die for us, resurrect Him, save us, and leave us to figure out how to solve life's problems? Jesus said our broken hearts, captivity, and woundedness are why He came. Why get entangled again in anything He delivers us from, my friend?

Ask the Lord for discernment when you encounter strange mental health techniques or encourage channeling to a vague deity or an outright idol. These may seem harmless, but the Bible clarifies how God feels about our hearts turning to other gods. We must be watchful of what our children are learning at school.

Sometimes, in the name of all-inclusiveness, children can be exposed to seemingly harmless counter-Christian coping techniques. Christian parents and grandparents are responsible for training the young to adhere to the faith and guide them to recognize subtle deviations that erode devotion to Christ.

Whatever is Lovely

DAY 4
NO COMPARISON!

*For our light and momentary troubles are
achieving for us an eternal glory that far
outweighs them all.*

— 2 CORINTHIANS 4:7

As I write this, I am struggling with something God wants me to do that I do not want to do. This is the second unwanted significant change He called me to this year. I have every intention of doing what He said because that is the life of the Christian. Our will must die so that we may live in Christ. My other emotions will catch up, but I am not yet happy. However, I have joy because I know I am pleasing the Father, which means more than anything. I have joy knowing I will not be ashamed when I stand before Him on that Day because, at least this time, I made the right choice.

Even in our disappointment at what God allows, we can trust He is up to something good. We may not see it yet, but we can be confident He will keep His promise to work all things for our good if we are His (Romans 8:28).

Think of your current trouble as a seed that will reap a harvest in eternity. Eternity will last longer than the most challenging days on Earth. Let's keep this perspective so that you do not lose heart. Some of the blessings will come before you breathe our last, and it is sweet of God to divide the spoils that way; however, you will be glad He did not give you all the rewards on this side of eternity.

Determine anew to live a life of obedience no matter the cost. The current suffering does not compare to the joy that awaits us. His blessings for obedience tip the scales overwhelmingly.

Think on these things.

Whatever Is Admirable

DAY 5
ENDURE POOR TREATMENT

*But how is it to your credit if you receive a
beating for doing wrong and endure it? But
if you suffer for doing good and you endure
it, this is commendable before God.*

— 1 PETER 2:20

Unbelievers do not understand us. We live by a different standard, which only makes sense to those who live it. Enduring poor treatment is counter-cultural and goes against human nature.

Retaliation and revenge are the typical responses to mistreatment, but Jesus calls us to a different one. We are to endure. This means we do not give up loving and praying for our enemies. This is impossible without the power of the Holy Spirit operating in us. Where does one's mindset need to be to endure?

The Apostle Peter lived when Christians were falsely accused and mistreated for living out their faith. They suffered persecution when they had done nothing wrong. Abandoning the faith was a temptation, but Peter encouraged them to remain steadfast.

This is not a call to be a doormat but a call to keep the faith when it hurts. Christ is our supreme example. He endured the cross because He knew our eternal destiny was at stake. We stay because the name of Christ is at stake. When we keep our joy in the face of all the enemy hurls at us, we glorify God, and people will be drawn to Him. None of us would choose to suffer, but sometimes, our only choice is to bear it or abandon the faith by conforming to the world.

If you are in a hard season that you need to endure, invite friends to pray for you so you do not lose heart. Jesus is with you and will strengthen you, my friend. Think on these things.

Whatever Is Morally Excellent

⤜⤛

DAY 6
CONFIDENTIALITY

A trustworthy person keeps a secret.

— PROVERBS 11:13

My first crush was on a boy named Clint in fifth grade. I told my best friend that I liked Clint and that she needed to keep this a secret. She told Clint, and I was so embarrassed! I remember how the betrayal hurt my young heart. My friend did not seem to care how she hurt me, which worsened everything.

Confidentiality is important because we all need someone to trust with our innermost feelings. God made us crave relationships, and sharing a secret creates a bond. Often, jealousy or malice is behind the divulgence of a secret. We look for someone to share in finding fault with the good fortune of someone who trusted us. Sin has marred how we interact with each other, but the presence of Christ in us should make us safe for friends to share their secrets with without fear of betrayal.

Jesus said to treat others as we wish to be treated (Matthew 7:12).

If someone starts a sentence with, "I was told not to tell you this, but..." you can be sure they will say the same to someone else behind your back. If you find yourself using these words, stop! Remember what Jesus said about doing to others the way you would have them do to you (Luke 6:31). If you want to have good friends, be a good one. Churches and offices seem to be fertile breeding grounds for breaking confidences. Hurt, anger, bitterness, and suspicion are some fruits that grow in these environments. As a follower of Christ, you must be a peacemaker, not an agitator. If you have been a traitor, repent and start fresh. Determine to be caught encouraging, praising, and being as silent as the grave when keeping confidences.

Whatever Is Worthy of Praise

❧

NEW EVERY MORNING

*His mercies never come to an end; they are new
every morning; great is your faithfulness.*

— LAMENTATIONS 3:22-23

The Bible says Job was wealthy and righteous, too. His response revealed his perspective about his life and possessions when disaster struck. He acknowledged that he came into the world with nothing and that he would leave the world with nothing. God gave everything to Job and had the divine right to take it away. That man blessed the name of the Lord. His wife did not have the same response to those hardships. She encouraged her husband to curse God and die.

Did she forget that her possessions, children, and health were gifts, not rights?

Fear of losing our blessings can make us paranoid if we are not careful. God has not promised loss will never happen, but He has promised that your greatest treasure, Himself, will never go away (Hebrews 13:5). Job knew the Lord would never leave

Him; therefore, He could praise the name of the Lord in the face of tragedy. You can, too.

Everyone faces a time when God takes back what He gave. Will you bless His name when your turn comes? Let the knowledge that God could recall His gifts at any moment inspire fresh gratitude for every day He lets you hold onto them. When you wake up and those blessings are still there, see them as intentional gifts from God. They are new every morning.

How do you keep the proper perspective about your blessings? Itemize them and thank Him for them each day. Like Job, enjoy every day to the fullest so that when they are gone, you have precious memories. Walk in joy and confidence that God's presence is always your best daily gift. Think on these things.

Whatever Is Pure

∽

DAY 8
STAY CLEAN!

*Come out from it and be pure, you who carry the
articles of the Lord's house.*

— ISAIAH 52:11

S ometimes, we forget how holy God is. True, God
declares us holy and blameless because of the blood of
Christ. Still, we must be consistent in confessing our
current sins to Him.

Unconfessed sin can harm our attitude and the way we treat
people. Confession keeps us humble and reminds us of our
dependence on God. It also makes us more sympathetic to the
struggles of others.

While sin can never condemn us, it can disrupt our inti-
mate fellowship with God. The flood of His Spirit's work can
become a trickle and leave us depending on our strength to
accomplish God's work. We also risk becoming careless in the
way we serve God.

We tend to give our best energies to our pursuits and give

God what is left when we neglect personal confession. We skip prayer and rely on the fumes of the last time we prayed. We are insensitive to the promptings of God's Spirit, relying on human reasoning and missing the opportunity to see God do what only He can.

Today's verse is a prophecy of deliverance for Jerusalem, but Isaiah mentioned that the priests were to purify themselves before handling the sacred objects of their ministry. Everything you do, Christian friend, is holy. You represent Christ every day because you bear His name.

Keep a clear conscience before God. Confession does not have to be a long, gut-wrenching process. Agree with what God points out to you and ask His forgiveness. He promises to cleanse you and restore fellowship. Are you clean today?

The devil loves to inflict false guilt. He deals with vagueness so that you feel guilty for nothing.

Remember, you only need cleansing from specific sins.

Whatever Is True

DAY 9
GOD DOES NOT NEED YOUR PERFECTION

*I can do all this through him who gives me
strength.*

— PHILIPPIANS 4:13

I wish I always thought the right thoughts and had the right attitude and motives. We both know that is only going to be true of all of us once we see Jesus. People hold back from coming to God because they fear failing God. Guess what? They will fail Him like we all do, even after receiving Christ. God does not need our perfection; He has plenty of His own. Your imperfections do not frighten or surprise Him. He is the One Who made you aware of your inadequacies in the first place. He provided His Son because you had no way of achieving perfection. His perfection covers your imperfections and is the only reason God can accept us into His family.

I saw a cute video on social media where a toddler sat in a laundry basket watching a video of a roller coaster ride. The adult behind the child made the basket dip and swerve in sync with the video. This is a picture of abiding in Christ. If you stay in the basket (abiding in Christ), you get to experience the power of Christ, enabling you to do amazing things. I have seen God use me to lead people to Christ when I was scared to death, forgive people who hurt me, and ask forgiveness when my pride wanted to remain silent. I have experienced the thrill of returning to school in my late 30s and watching God provide to honor my commitment to graduate debt- free. Was I perfect in any of those ventures? Absolutely not! Christ in us is the secret, not perfection.

Are you holding back on your God-given assignment because you cannot do it perfectly?

Whatever Is Right

BELIEVE GOD!

*And without faith it is impossible to please
God because anyone who comes to him must
believe that he exists and that he rewards
those who earnestly seek him.*

— HEBREWS 13:5

Believing in God is not the same as believing Him. Believing in Him is acknowledging His existence. He wants more from you than that, my friend. God wants you to believe what He says and show it.

Believe Him when He says you are forgiven through Jesus Christ. Show it by refusing to look down on yourself because of your past. Believe God when He says

He will provide for you. Show your belief by doing your part, knowing He will do His. Show it by refusing to be jealous of anyone else. You have all you need in Him, which frees you to rejoice at how He blesses others. Show it by being generous, knowing God will meet your needs when you care for others. Belief without action is empty.

Believe God when He says He is in control. Show your faith by waiting for His timing. Command your heart to be still when tempted to manipulate things to get your way. Trust me, you don't want it if you must steal it and miss God's best, my friend.

Believing God is a form of worship. You exalt His character and echo everything He has said about Himself. Faith always excited Jesus when He saw it (Matthew 8:5-10; Mark 7:24-30).

Believing God makes you behave in ways that make no sense to unbelievers.

That's OK. You are in good company with Noah, Joshua, and Mary, the mother of Jesus. The world has nothing better to offer than the life of faith does. Know this!

Believe this! Believe God!

Whatever is Admirable

∽

DAY 11

STARVE GREED!

Watch out! Be on your guard against all kinds of greed.

— LUKE 12:15

We usually think of money when greed comes up, but we can be greedy with our time.

Some would rather write a hefty check than give their time. Many choose to keep their schedule open in case something better comes up rather than commit to serving even an hour a month. I have been to many churches where a small percentage of the congregation serves the majority who hoard their time. We are all members of each other, and the whole Body suffers when any part fails to do its share.

The call to share our time with others challenges the selfishness and laziness in each of us. The devil strategically capitalizes on these tendencies. He knows that if we love others to the point of serving them, we will grow to be more like Christ, and the kingdom of God will advance. He wants to keep us weak and ineffective because the kingdom of darkness already has significant real estate in the hearts and minds of people. Our apathy only helps advance the devil's work! He does not want us to stand before God and be rewarded for being a faithful servant. He entices us with distractions and fears that serving others makes us poorer. Nothing could be farther from the truth. We discover that we get more enormous blessings when we seek to bless others.

Every family seems to have at least one member who always needs help but has yet to be available to help anyone. The Body of Christ is a family, too. Are you more of a consumer than a contributor at your church? Ask the Lord to show you how to starve greed in your life. Think on these things.

Whatever is Lovely

DAY 12
GIVE HIM GLORY

The LORD has done this, and it is marvelous in
our eyes.

— PSALM 118:23

I know a woman whom God rescued from a long life of bondage. Her joy is contagious! Even when she's not speaking, I've seen her burst into a giggle because she is so glad her life is turned around. Most of us have at least one significant act that God did that we can never get over. Maybe God healed you or a loved one of a disease. Perhaps your marriage was nearly over, and then God transformed the relationship. Maybe your Red Sea story involves deliverance from an addiction no one thought you'd overcome. Your salvation may be the theme of your heart's song. Our stories are lovely because they touch a particular part of us and remind us how much God cares. His power was manifested in our weakness, and we have never been the same.

Unbelievers may experience similar miracles, but they give

credit to something or someone else. You and I know the Lord is behind every gift, and we must be careful to shower Him with grateful praise. The heart of God rejoices when we acknowledge and glorify Him for His magnificent work. Can you ever thank Him enough for what He's done for you? Ongoing praise is appropriate for such fantastic deliverance.

I knew another woman with three of her four sons enslaved to drugs simultaneously. She talked about how she fasted and lay prostrate with her nose in the carpet, praying for their deliverance. When God did it many years later, she practically shouted as she recalled what the Lord had done. She recounted what the Lord did with great adoration at every opportunity to testify. He wants the same from you. Give Him glory!

Whatever Is Admirable

DAY 13
LOYALTY

*Know therefore that the LORD your God, He is
God, the faithful God, who keeps His
covenant and His lovingkindness to a thou-
sandth generation with those who love Him
and keep His commandments.*

— DEUTERONOMY 7:9

L oyalty is worthy of respect. It is hard to find because
our sinful nature wants to be loyal only to itself.
When things are good, commitment is easy, but
loyalty is more of a challenge when they go badly. It thinks of
the other person more than itself. It has the scent of grace
because loyalty is not always deserved. It is a gift we give because
of love or because it is the right thing to do. Loyalty may cost
you something because it sometimes means you take a loss for
the good of the other person. Loyalty stays when everyone else
leaves.

Loyalty to Christ is to stay in line with His will instead of our own. It means that kingdom business is to be paramount in our lives. He promises that if we are loyal to His mission, He will supply all our needs. (Matthew 6:33).

Loyalty is a beautiful characteristic of God's love. Wherever the Bible mentions the Lord's "lovingkindness" or "faithfulness," loyalty is part of its meaning. God's lovingkindness never forgets its promises. His loyal love promises never to abandon you, so you never need to feel insecure about the unknown. In this life, people break vows, leaving us feeling alone, angry, and devastated. The loyal love of God will sustain you, my friend. When you feel misunderstood, falsely accused, or that evil seems to win out, forgive and let Christ's loyalty to you comfort you.

How has the Lord been loyal to you? In what way is He calling you to be faithful to Him and others?

Think On This

⁓

God can make you sick enough of what you settled for to confront what you have been fearing.

Think On This

~

One prayer
is better than
a thousand nags

Whatever Is of Moral Excellence

DAY 14
ZERO SEXUAL IMMORALITY

But among you, there must not be even a hint of
sexual immorality.

— EPHESIANS 5:3

You may have to ride in the middle of the road to avoid falling into a ditch. It is better to overdo it in prevention to avoid catastrophe than to see how close you can get without failing. Sexual immorality is like that. Single Christians face great difficulty remaining sexually pure, and the culture acts as if it is impossible, but it is not.

Fill your mind with media that focus on wholesome pursuits. Do not fall for the lie that this means boredom. God has created a vast world full of many things to learn and discover. Ask Him to show you what He has prepared for you to enjoy. Occupy yourself with music, books, and people who encourage you to live for Christ. Memorize Scripture and meditate on it in those moments when temptation is high.

Keep a humble attitude about how much you can endure

in your strength. Never underestimate the power of your flesh, my friend. Sin succeeds because a magnet inside us is attracted to what we know is not right. Rely on all the spiritual and practical resources available to protect yourself sexually. Flirting with a married man can open the door to immorality. Please don't do it!

Establish boundaries. Determine what places and scenarios will not be part of your lifestyle, and do not compromise them for anyone. Find friends who share your values and establish mutual accountability.

You can do all things through Christ, including abstaining from sexual sin. Nothing is worth the regret and other consequences that accompany poor choices. For the glory of God, be vigilant in your resolve that not even a hint of sexual immorality will be part of your life.

Whatever Is Worthy of Praise

❦

DAY 15
GOD IS ON YOUR SIDE

The LORD is with me; I will not be afraid.
What can mere mortals do to me?

— PSALM 118:6

The Lord is worthy of praise because He is on your side! If God is for you, what does it matter if anyone is against you? When I was young, I wished for an older brother. As the oldest girl, I was expected to protect my sisters. It seemed everyone wanted to fight, and I was always afraid. A male cousin came to live with our family for a while, and I hoped he would defend me against the bullies, but he did not. I longed to have someone on my side who would fight the battles I was too scared to fight. Have you ever felt this way? The environment at your job may be contentious. Perhaps you need help to stay out of the family drama. You wish you had someone on your side.

It may sound awkward, but my friend, the Lord is on your

side. He wants you to know He is there to listen to you and give you wisdom on what to do in uncomfortable situations.

His Holy Spirit living inside you can enable you to exercise self-control in heated situations. He will provide you with His peace when chaos surrounds you.

When you are wrong, He will give you grace to admit it. He will help you remain calm and choose your words with clarity. He is on your side because He loves you, and you represent Him in the middle of complex situations. He will never leave you to figure everything out by yourself. He will even tell you when it is time to remain silent. He is your most faithful Friend. For all of this, He is worthy of praise.

Whatever Is True

DAY 16

YOU CAN CHOOSE NOT TO STRESS

Cast all your anxiety on him because he cares for you.

—1 PETER 5:7

My friend, you do not have to be at the mercy of your circumstances. Yes, you have a lot to do, and you feel overwhelmed. You are only one person, and you cannot do it all. Ask God to give you His perspective on your day. He will! Jesus never stressed when He was going about His days on earth. His heart became troubled when He was about to experience the cross, but He did not wring His hands in anxiety about His daily schedule. You can be the same way. You can choose to offer this day up to God. Tell Him all you need to do, then surrender your list to Him.

Tell Him that you want to do what He says is most important. You will discover that God cares about the details of your day. He will give you His perspective and unique brand of peace. He will show you what can wait for another day.

I did a prayer event for a ministry I worked at years ago. There was always so much work and a small window of time to do it. I was amazed at how God provided people I did not know to drop by and help. He made everything come together beautifully. He wants to do the same in stressful situations. He wants you to hand every detail over to Him and let Him do His beautiful work. It will save you a lot of anxiety, fill you with awe at how God works, and strengthen your faith.

What anxieties will you hand over to God today? Do you trust Him enough to adjust your "to-do" list today? Think on these things.

Whatever is Right

DAY 17

REMEMBER TO PRAY

*... but in everything, by prayer and petition, with
thanksgiving, present your requests to God.*

— PHILIPPIANS 4:6

Sometimes, we forget to pray. We talk to our friends and research the internet about our problems before we remember to speak with our Heavenly Father about them. You have a standing invitation to talk to Him about everything. Are you struggling with a child or your spouse? Tell God all about it. Ask for His wisdom. Are you worried about your grandchild or a friend at work? Taking their problems to God is one of the most loving things you can do. Need to know the best way to arrange your day? Ask God. He loves when you invite Him into every area of your life. Need help with your temper, your attitude, or controlling your eating? God says to hurl all of this on Him through prayer.

Sometimes, I forget to pray, and I worry instead. I stress about what to cook for dinner. I worry about my adult children and about not getting everything done. I recall coming home from work one day, and my chest was in a knot. I had so many concerns on my mind, and I felt overwhelmed. Then God reminded me I had not talked to Him about any of it, so I prayed. I itemized everything, yes, every single burden. It took a while because there was a lot in my heart, but the knot was gone when I finished. Peace took its place, and I was grateful. God wants to do the same for you.

What have you been worrying about lately but have forgotten to pray about?

Is there anything on your mind big enough to worry about that you think is too small to pray about? Remember to pray.

Whatever Is Pure

DAY 18
HOW GOD SEES YOU

*But now he has reconciled you by Christ's physical
body through death to present you holy in his
sight, without blemish and free from
accusation.*

— COLOSSIANS 1:22

What area of your life do you find most challenging to see yourself as God sees you? Today, celebrate that because of Christ, God sees you as pure, holy, and blameless.

The more acquainted you become with your sinful nature, the higher the hallelujah for what the blood of Christ has done for God's view of you.

We look just like Jesus. He sees no sin, no guilt, no cause for shame. It is as if your past was perfect, your present is unsullied, and your future is flawless.

Nothing can ever change this, my friend. When Christ said,

"It is finished," your right standing with God was sealed. This is cause for eternal rejoicing.

How does this make you respond to Christ? Does it make you want to sin as much as possible because you know you are under the blood of Christ? May it never be! The brutal price that Christ paid for our sins should make us want to please Him. He did it all so that we could enjoy reconciliation. Would you mistreat someone who saved your child or mother from a burning building? What could they ask of you that you would not give with your whole heart, considering what they did for you? God did what He did so that you could have access to Him and He to you. A holy life is not too much to offer Him. Bless His name! Praise Him forever for the permanent purity He accounts to us.

May we live a life of gratitude and holiness in response to such great love.

Whatever Is Lovely

DAY 19

GENTLENESS

Do not rebuke an older man harshly, but exhort
him as if he were your father. Treat younger
men as brothers, older women as mothers,
and younger women as sisters, with absolute
purity.

— 1 TIMOTHY 5:1-2

Sometimes, it is not what you say but how you say it that is the problem. Confrontation is part of life, but rude roughness does not have to be. The Golden Rule applied here will save your reputation and the feelings of others. What tone would you prefer someone use to correct you? Maybe your feelings are made of tougher stuff but recognize that not everyone's are. How would you desire Jesus to handle you when you are wrong?

Notice that today's Bible verses do not say we are to avoid correcting others.

Insecurity wants to avoid all confrontation, even at the

expense of what is right, but Christ calls us to love each other enough to say what needs saying but with gentleness. Gentleness is a fruit of the Spirit, meaning you have His power to be gentle if you belong to Jesus. Practice your words before you approach the other person if you fear you may be indelicate. Ask the Lord to give you the words that preserve the other person's dignity while imparting vital information.

I had a boss who needed to correct me about an issue. She was so gentle in the way she did it that only in retrospect did I realize she was reprimanding me. No doubt she asked God to give her the gentleness she needed to approach me about this slightly embarrassing situation. You have the same help at your disposal, my friend. Gentleness is an amiable quality in a world where rudeness and humiliation are common. Seize the opportunity to be like Jesus through gentleness.

Whatever Is Worthy of Respect

❧

DAY 20

FOOT-WASHING 101

*If I then, your Lord and Master, have washed
your feet; ye also ought to wash one another's
feet.*

— JOHN 13:14-15

When Jesus washed the disciples' feet, does it occur to you that he could identify each disciple just by looking at their feet? He also knew that Peter's feet would run in betrayal and Judas's would dangle when he hung himself. Christ washed the feet of each disciple, knowing He would not get a perfect return on His investment in them. He taught them the vulnerability of service.

It is human to want to reap abundance from every seed you plant. How wonderful it would be if every soul you shared the gospel with eventually, if not immediately, came to Christ. If you focus on what you may lose, you will die of discouragement, hoard your gifts, or live going crazy.

I have served in a few non-profit ministries. It bothered me when people took advantage of services by being wasteful or taking more than they needed. Some would stay around long enough to get all the expensive stuff for free and then leave unchanged. I was frustrated until the Lord taught me that He knew they would squander those gifts before He offered them, and He gave them anyway. He reminded me those were HIS resources, and they would always stay supplied. My job was to be a faithful servant and leave the results with Him. Their misuse did not affect my reward. I eventually learned that sometimes people look back after a long time and realize the grace they received all those years ago. Even wasted things can glorify God.

Just as Christ washed the disciples' feet with full knowledge that He could suffer loss, you and I must serve, knowing we risk much but gain more. Think on these things.

Whatever Is of Moral Excellence

‿‿

DAY 21
CLEAN LANGUAGE

What goes into someone's mouth does not defile them, but what comes out of their mouth, that is what defiles them.

— MATTHEW 15:11

What comes out of your mouth reveals what is in your heart. The goal is not just to say the right things but to have the heart change that makes those words pure. Cussing is one of those sins often Christians excuse. It is so common that it seems futile to try to stop it. If you used profanity a lot before becoming a Christian, you may find it challenging to control, especially when angry. Keep in mind that your words reflect Christ to those around you. Most people know that cussing is wrong, so when they see you do it, what conclusion will they draw about Jesus?

I encourage you to purpose in your heart to keep your language clean. Enlist an accountability partner, and your chances of success will increase. Write down every time you let a cuss word slip. You may be surprised at how often you cuss without realizing it.

We all are on the road to Christlikeness. Do not condemn yourself for this sin, but do not make excuses either. Confess the sin every time, and God will forgive you. Ask Him to clean your language up by changing your heart. Ask Him to reveal why you use foul language. Is it to gain respect? Is it your weapon when afraid? Does it make you feel confident? Does it make you feel more adult? It could be a matter of poor self-control. Any reason you find is a poor substitute for what you have in Christ, my friend.

Jesus wants you to represent Him well in every area of life for His glory. This includes your language. Think on these things.

Whatever Is Worthy of Praise

DAY 22
GOD RESTORES JOY

You make known to me the path of life; in your presence there is fullness of joy; at your right hand are pleasures forevermore.

— PSALM 16:11

How would your life change if you remembered you were always in the presence of God? He is always aware of you, and your awareness of His presence affects everything! How would you view your troubles as you recognize He is there with you in them? Would it change your perspective on your inadequacies to know God knew what He was getting when He saved you? His plan all along was to be strong in your weakness!

Do you see God as always scowling and rolling His eyes at you? His love for you is unconditional, and if you are His, this will draw you to love Him back, not drive you to take unholy advantage of it.

You can go nowhere that He cannot find you, my friend.

Rejoice that He never wants His child to feel alone. He brings His omnipotence and love everywhere, so you always have the resources to do His will.

Today's verse reminds us that complete joy is found in the presence of God. How might that joy be lost? When our sin makes us want to hide from Him or when we are angry that He acted contrary to our preference, joy escapes us. What then? How do we restore that joy?

We come out of hiding, confess, and repent. The pathway to joy is paved with renewing surrender, reminding ourselves we are not in control. The Lord knows what He's doing. When He tells you the path to life, joy comes when you follow it.

How is your joy today? What might you need to do to restore it?

Whatever is True

❧

YOU CANNOT CHANGE PEOPLE

So then, each of us will give an account of
ourselves to God.

— ROMANS 14:12

G od has gifted you in many ways, but the ability to change another person is not one of them.

We sometimes go into a relationship thinking we will change another person's habits. People change because they decide to change. They determine that staying the way they are is uncomfortable enough to do something different. Your nagging is not enough to make them change. Nagging makes them more determined to stay the same because they do not want anyone to control them.

God is the only One with the power to change people, and He rarely does it against their will. If you love someone who needs to make essential changes, you have two roles: prayer and influence. Prayer is asking God to do what only He can do. You can be sure that God will also change you while you pray. Influence is the ability to impact the person who needs to change. It is not manipulation. It is behaving in a way that encourages someone to conclude that they must make different choices if they want better outcomes. This takes wisdom and patience on your part.

When I served in a recovery facility, the most successful clients grew tired of their lives enough to do whatever it took to make a better life. Those forced into recovery resented being there, made excuses, and were not yet convinced they needed to change. It can be hard to wait for people to draw the correct conclusions for change, but it is better than wasting energy trying to make those decisions for them. Love them, pray for them, influence them, but give up trying to change them. That is not your job.

Whatever Is True

⤳

YOU HAVE ALREADY WON

*No, in all these things we are more than
conquerors through him who loved us.*

— ROMANS 8:37

I love all the "through Him's" in Scripture. Philippians 4:13 promises that you and I can do all things through Christ. We Christians have the gift of eternal life through Christ according to Romans 6:23. Today's verse is one I must pause to think about, however. Some days I do not feel like a conqueror or an overcomer, but God says I am more than a conqueror. It is not because of anything I offer, but this victory is through Christ.

What is threatening to overcome you today, my friend? Guilt? Insecurity? Unforgiveness? An aggravating coworker? Whatever it is, you have already won because God has provided what you need through Christ.

How does this truth become a reality in your life? For example, if you have financial struggles today that feel like they have overcome you, how does the victory you have in Christ apply? The answer is by faith! God has promised to provide all your needs, but you do not yet see it. You must trust that God will do what He promised. Daily He gives you the grace to get through your needy season. He offers ideas on how to make money, connections to find work, and strength to do your job.

Faith does not mean it will be easy. Overcoming is often a journey. Knowing that Christ is right there with you means you will reach your destination if you stay with Him. It is like being in a fight where the outcome is already determined, but you must get into the ring to win. Go through today acting as if you have already won because, in Christ, you have! Think on this.

Whatever is Right

DAY 25
AVOIDANCE

In your anger do not sin.

— EPHESIANS 4:26

S ometimes, the right thing to do involves avoiding something. When you are angry, avoid speaking too quickly. Think about your words before you say them.

They can be forgiven but never forgotten once you say them. Also, ask questions to clarify instead of assuming you already know everything. Misunderstandings do happen. I'll never forget the day a father came storming into the high school library demanding to know why a lost library book threatened his daughter's graduation.

He was loud and disruptive. The librarian looked up the student's file and explained that there was no lost book; his daughter only needed to pay a fine for an overdue book, and her grades would be released, and she could graduate.

Avoid bringing up the past. If you have not forgiven them, work to do so.

Avoid making important decisions when you are angry. Anger is like a drug, and you are not at your best when intoxicated by it.

Avoid physical violence. It is better to leave the scene if you feel you cannot control yourself than to suffer the consequences of violence.

Avoid spreading strife. (Provers 6:19). Enlist the help of a mediator if you cannot resolve the problem, but avoid involving too many people outside the situation.

This could lead to gossip and taking sides. The biblical model is to attempt to work it out with the individual and gradually bring others in as needed (Matthew 18:15-17).

Avoid accusations. State how their actions made you feel instead of attacking their character or assuming you know their motives. This puts them on the defensive, distracting them from resolving the problem. Ask the Holy Spirit to take control when angry to avoid regrets.

Avoidance is not cowardice. It is wisdom. Think on these things.

Whatever is Pure

❦

DAY 26

STOCK UP!

I have hidden your word in my heart that I
might not sin against you.

— PSALM 119:11

In today's verse, "hidden" has been translated as "treasured" and can also mean "to stock up." My grandmother had a garden, and I remember seeing her deep freezer stocked with vegetables she had grown. Like my grandmother, we stock up on what we will need for the future. How do you stock up God's Word in your heart?

Every time you read the Word of God, you are stocking up on the knowledge you need. The Words will not jump off the page daily, which is ok. Often, God gives us truths that strengthen a part of us we did not know was weak.

Do not wait until troubles come before you start reading your Bible. Do not quit reading it when life is hard. Do not allow busyness to be an excuse to keep you from the Word. Make the intake of Scripture a daily habit, like eating. When reading the Word seems dry, ask the Lord to moisten it (Psalm 119:18). Try reading in a different translation. Research the answer to a Bible question you have always wondered about, or look up all the verses that contain a specific word. Like broccoli, there are many ways to serve yourself the Word. The point is to make sure you get it in.

Why go to all the trouble to stock up on the Word? It is so that we may not sin against the Lord. The Scriptures purify. God's Word will get you through messy emotions and help you to love messy people. We want to make Him smile; obedience is the best way to do it. Obedience comes from a stocked-up heart, so stock up on truth every day.

Whatever Is Lovely

DAY 27

WHEN FRIENDSHIPS DIE

*... love your enemies and pray for those who perse-
cute you.*

— MATTHEW 5:44

The end of a friendship is a sad reality, even among Christians. Despite all the supernatural resources available, sometimes relationships go beyond repair. Forgiveness is always in order, but reconciliation may not be. The damage to trust may be too extensive to remain in proximity. The road back to open vulnerability may require more time than you have left on earth.

How do you keep your heart soft without becoming a doormat when this happens? How do you move on even when it hurts? Prayer and love from a distance are the keys, my friend. It is difficult to be bitter while ministering to someone through intercessory prayer. Be sure to pray God's will for them, not what you think they need. Every time they come to mind, let your prayers for them outrun the reels of hurt you are tempted to replay. Place them in the Lord's hands and trust Him to do what is necessary. People around you may not understand why the friendship must end. They may misunderstand why their simple answers do not fit your situation. You do not have to clear their conscience about your decision if yours is clear before God.

Love from a distance may look cruel, but sometimes healing happens best when you are far enough away to stop the cycle of reinjury (Proverbs 27:12). If your former friend has a need God calls you to meet, do it knowing that reuniting does not have to be part of the package. Acknowledge your part in the relationship breakdown and refuse to live under condemnation.

Walk in the same forgiveness you offered them and allow the experience to fortify future friendships. Think on these things.

Whatever Is of Moral Excellence

∽

DAY 28

HUMILITY

Live in harmony with one another. Do not be proud but be willing to associate with people of low position. Do not be conceited.

— ROMANS 12:16

Humility is hard to find but beautiful when you see it. People fear humility because they think it means vulnerability to exploitation. They also fear it means losing opportunities. These things are valid if no God exists, but His presence makes humility safe.

Today's verse warns against pride. Have you ever been embarrassed that someone saw you with someone who did not fit in? Jesus surrounded Himself with the outcasts of society. He was there to love and serve them even though He was the Son of God.

Scripture commands us to humble ourselves in the sight of the Lord. How do you do that? It starts with realizing we are nothing special and someone special at the same time.

We are nothing special because we are sinners relying on the same grace as everyone else. We are something special because the One Who is above everyone else loves us. Both truths should keep us humble. Pride builds fences that say certain people should keep out. Humility says that all are welcome, have value, and need God's same grace.

An uncle once posed this question: If I was working with a group of people to dig a hole with our bare hands and there was no water to wash hands when it was time to eat, whose hands would I prohibit from passing me a sandwich? We all dug from the same dirt; therefore, no one person's hands were dirtier than another's. The same is true with humility. We all are imperfect from God's view. We all need the same grace. Pride has no place in any heart!

Whatever Is Worthy of Praise

❦

KEEP GOD'S PRIORITIES

But seek first his kingdom and his righteousness,
and all these things will be given to you as
well.

— MATTHEW 6:33

I f you want to hear God say, "Well done, good and faithful servant," His priorities must be yours. As Christians, we can be busy without being productive. We can work at the expense of the most important things. Jesus said that if we first seek His kingdom and righteousness, all the other things we strive for will be added. This is the opposite of the way our natural mind works.

We tend to think that if we get a lot of money in the bank and the big house first, we can be free to do great things for God. Nothing is wrong with aspiring to have more; we must ensure that God's agenda does not defer to ours. Jesus said we should not worry about our basic needs because He has promised to provide them. The problem comes when we do not budget our time, energy, and money, so the Kingdom has prime real estate in all three areas. Let us not take the resources God gives and hoard them for ourselves while His priorities go unaccomplished.

This does not mean we all have to quit our jobs, sell all our possessions, and feed people experiencing poverty daily. No, Satan likes to suggest extremes to repel you. God's way is often to incorporate Kingdom giving and Kingdom work into the rhythm of your life. This looks like giving God off the top of your income instead of what is left over. It means serving as a lifestyle.

In what ways might God be calling you to adjust your life so that His priorities are yours, too?

Whatever Is True

DAY 30
YOU ARE NEVER ALONE

*Where can I go to escape Your Spirit? Where can
I flee from Your presence?*

— PSALM 139:7

Even if you feel alone, know that you never are. Your emotions do not tell you the truth if you feel alone. God would have to stop being omnipresent for you to be alone, my friend. Not only is God present everywhere, but He is also everywhere all the time. When He says He will never leave you, He means it. Others may promise never to desert you, but they have limited power to honor that promise. Death and unexpected circumstances may hinder their ability, but God sits above the circumstances. He is eternal, and death cannot overtake Him. Know that wherever you are, God is with you. He is rejoicing in your happy seasons, comforting you in your sad ones, and offering His presence when confusion darkens your days. The Psalmist reminds us that "God is our refuge and strength, an ever-present help in trouble" (Psalm 46:1).

When devastation occurs at your house, you may feel numb with the shock. Do not mistake that numbness for the absence of God. He designed the mind and body to withstand trauma for protection. Know that God is holding you in your dazed state. When you cannot think of a single

Scripture to comfort you, know that their truth is not dependent on your memory. They are true because God is faithful. When you look for Him but struggle to understand what has happened, know His presence is better than any answer. He has not promised to explain. He promised never to let you go through the unexplained by yourself. His grace is sufficient. Rejoice in this truth and let it settle your heart. Know this truth and let it make you free!

Whatever Is Noble

DAY 31

HUMAN LIFE

You shall not murder.

— EXODUS 20:13

I recall passing a dead dog on my way home. Had it been a person, authorities would have been called. Why? Because human life is precious. Not to say we don't love animals, but human life is different. Why do you suppose people need counseling after killing in the line of duty? Why is a newborn placed in a trashcan to die unthinkable? Why do you think God said, "Do not kill"? Human life is precious!

Think back to the darkest times in history when the color of a person's skin or ethnicity deemed them unworthy of respect and dignity. Mass murders became acceptable when people were regarded as mere animals or less than animals. We call people who do such things criminals. Notice, however, that messages are coming through media and entertainment that say human life is dispensable if it is inconvenient or imperfect. As a crisis pregnancy center counselor, I saw the importance of godly family members and friends speaking about the value of human life early and often. Those with early biblical moorings were less likely to terminate a pregnancy or had a voice in their head convicting them about their plans. The culture's messages start early, and so must we, my friend. Please do not assume kids know what is right about this.

My experience also prompts me to encourage you never to declare or imply that an unplanned pregnancy is an unpardonable sin. You would be shocked to know how many innocent lives have been lost to protect the pride and reputation of the family. In the face of this life-changing event, grace can save a life and a woman's emotional health. It also avoids having to account to God for having a hand in taking a life.

Whatever Is Right

DAY 32

FORGIVE YOURSELF

Who will bring any charge against those whom
God has chosen? It is God who justifies.

— ROMANS 8:33

Unforgiveness is like acid; it eats away at you and hinders God's work in your life because it is a sin. It is not worth it, my friend. Forgiving others can be challenging, but forgiving yourself can be harder—unless. Unless you see it for the sin that it is, you may be tempted to believe that not forgiving yourself is humble. It is the opposite. Not forgiving yourself is mistreating someone God loves. It is pride because you act as if your sin is more terrible than anyone else's and deserves more grace than everyone else's. Yes!

Imagine God inviting everyone to throw their sins into the fire of forgiveness. People come in droves, casting their sins into the fire and enjoying the freedom of getting that guilt and shame off their shoulders. Everyone comes to the fire but you. Jesus looks at you and says, "You are hiding a sin that needs to go into the fire." You answer that it is because you think it is too ugly and you are too ashamed. Jesus then tells you that you have insulted Him and acted like the blood He shed on the cross was not powerful enough. You are acting as if your sin is special. Jesus then says your refusal to forgive yourself in agreement with what He says is disrespect.

"Whoa! I was not saying that at all," you say. Jesus replies, "But that is how I see it. If I declare you forgiven, not forgiving yourself is contradicting Me. "

Throw the sin of holding a grudge against yourself into the fire today. Say aloud, "Lord, I forgive myself out of respect for your sacrifice!"

Think On This

⌒⌒⌒

The hardest thing
to stop when you're
scared is doing
nothing to change.

Think On This

Jealousy
is an accusation
against the Almighty

Whatever Is Pure

DAY 33
WORD OF GOD

*Every word of God is flawless; he is a shield to
those who take refuge in him.*

— PROVERBS 30:5

D o you know people who, if their lips are moving, you know they are lying? You cannot be sure of anything they say, and what a frustration this is. Sometimes their words sound so good that you wish you could believe them. Many women have suffered a broken heart due to the lies of a man who said he loved her, but his actions proved otherwise. Men have suffered the same from lying women. Politicians make promises during campaigns but break them after winning the election.

In contrast, the Word of God is flawless. He can't lie (Hebrews 6:18). If He has said it, you can believe it. He will do whatever He promised. His Word is as sure as His character. Knowing you can trust it brings joy when reading His Word.

You never have to second-guess what He said. You never need to worry about it changing.

God's Word is a gift, my friend, so read it, study it, and let it give you peace. The Scriptures address every need because its Author knew beforehand what to provide for His children. If ever you think you see a contradiction, know that it means you need clarification. Ask Him to open your eyes to understanding (Psalm 119:18). You will be a lifetime student of the pure Word because the One Who wrote it is infinite. Of course, some passages will remain hard to understand, but you will discover far more beauty and truth than mystery. You will grow in character and love for Him.

The Author is pure, His Word is pure, and so is His love for you. Think about these things.

Whatever Is Lovely

DAY 34
AN ENCOURAGING WORD

... and how good is a timely word!

— PROVERBS 15:23

I t is a mistake to assume the people in your life know what a difference they make in your life.

Even if they do, no one gets tired of hearing it said. Because people are more apt to complain, a word of encouragement can lift them more than you know. You can never go wrong spreading sunshine wherever you go. People will not tell you, but they need to know they make a difference.

I remember in college, a beautiful girl who always looked put together got a new hairdo. It was a dramatic change that suited her attractive features. Well into the day, she sat at a table where a line of students took turns having her serve them. The person in front of me complimented her hairdo. She brightened and looked surprised and relieved. She said that no one had said anything about it all day and that she had begun to wonder if the new look had been a mistake. I assumed that she had received several compliments by that time of day and would not need mine, but I learned that day always to offer a good word whenever I can.

Does a color look good on the receptionist at the bank? Tell her. If the service at your favorite drive-thru restaurant is always fast and friendly, let them know. I suspect we all assume people know what a good job they are doing or that others have already told them. People are generally hard on themselves, and your encouragement could brighten their day. Never miss an opportunity to express lovely thoughts to increase the number of people around you who have a lovely day. Let God use you in this way. You'll be glad!

Whatever Is Noble

DAY 35
RESPECT HUMAN AUTHORITY

*Everyone must submit himself to the governing
authorities, for there is no authority except
that which God has established. The authorities that exist have been established by God.*

— ROMANS 13:1

I have observed that many struggle to respect human authority. It is as though being told what to do has to mean inferiority. It does not. Respecting human authority is about order, not worth. If you respect God's authority, then you ought to, in obedience to God, respect human authority. When one of our kids was young, he grew frightened whenever he saw a police car. Puzzled at such a strong reaction, we asked questions and discovered that this fear stemmed from watching a popular reality television show with his grandmother. We explained there was no need to fear since he was not a law-breaking preschooler.

I realize this is simplistic, considering the discrimination and brutality that has come to light recently, but the general principle remains the same. God places boundaries on our behavior through speed limits, traffic lights, and city ordinances. As children of God, you and I are called to obey the laws of the land if they do not contradict the laws of God. Are you an example others should follow? Do you purchase bootleg movies and music? Do you text while driving?

Every law we violate has the potential to hurt someone, even if we do not personally know the victim. Ask God to search your life and heart for ways you may dismiss the law because it serves you or because no one else seems to care to obey it. James 4:17 warns, "If anyone, then, knows the good they ought to do and doesn't do it, it is sin."

Growth will happen when you respect human authority. Think on these things.

Whatever Is Right

DAY 36

REST!

*Come with me by yourselves to a quiet place and
get some rest.*

— MARK 6:31

I was a stressed-out full-time mother of three, and one weekend, my husband took all three boys away on a road trip for two days. The first night, I was so wound up I could not relax. I had been "on" for too long, and my body had forgotten how to decompress. I reclined my body, but my mind was still racing. I was suffering from SCSD, Small Children Stress Disorder, if that is a thing. I worried I would not wind down before they returned the next day. After several hours, I fell asleep. The next day, I was better. I never wanted to get burnt out like that again. Can you relate? Do you feel like a hamster on that little wheel, always working and meeting your family's needs? It is good to be industrious, and having someone to care for feels good, but you must take care of yourself, too.

I learned, especially when I began homeschooling, to make time for myself, or I would not be suitable for anyone. There was a stoop outside my back door where I took a book to sit and read, even for a few minutes. On the weekends, I spread a quilt out under a tree in the backyard after warning my children not to disturb me unless somebody was bleeding. My kids are grown now, but I still must be intentional about making time for myself. This means saying "no" to some lovely opportunities for the sake of my emotional and mental health. I learned that making time for myself is caring for somebody God loves. You are somebody God loves, too, so take the time to refresh your beautiful self.

Whatever Is Noble

DAY 37

NO TWO WAYS ABOUT IT

*So I say, walk by the Spirit, and you will not
gratify the desires of the flesh.*

— GALATIANS 5:16

Y ou cannot walk north and south at the same time. Driving a car in two different directions simultaneously is impossible. You must choose which way you will go.

The same is true of walking in the Spirit versus fulfilling the desires of the flesh.

Any Christian who decides to do her own thing is automatically not going to do God's will. The flesh and the Spirit want what is contrary to each other, so there is no middle ground. Making one choice cancels out the other.

Have you ever met a Christian who tries to live for Jesus while following the world's values? How would you describe her? The Bible describes them as carnal or fleshly. Do you think a carnal Christian will fulfill her purpose? Will she impact her circle of influence for the glory of God? How effective are her claims to know Christ among her friends, unsaved family members, and community? Will she hear the Lord call her a good, faithful servant or a wicked, lazy one?

You can be sure your days will brim with new adventures when you choose to walk in the Spirit. It starts in your mind. You must have what they call a "made-up mind," a consistent resolve to submit yourself to the Holy Spirit in every aspect of your day. It will not happen by accident, my friend. You must decide your direction in your mind, heart, attitude, and relationships. When you slip (as we all do) immediately confess the infraction, believe you have forgiveness, and keep going.

You have two choices. How will you decide to live today?

Whatever Is Worthy of Praise

֍

DAY 38

HOPE WHEN THE WORST HAPPENS

*Dear friends, do not be surprised at the fiery
ordeal that has come on you to test you as
though something strange were happening
to you.*

— 1 PETER 4:12

Job had lost his family and health when he said, "What I feared has come upon me; what I dreaded has happened to me" (Job 3:25). Sometimes nightmares come true. Nobody likes to talk about this, but it is a truth we are wise to understand. The Christian life does not insulate us from nightmares. God has made no promise that nothing bad will ever happen to us. Jesus warned that trouble is a guarantee in this life.

I was talking to a loved one who was frustrated with his life. He was angry with God for the trials that seemed non-stop. When I reminded him that knowing Jesus did not mean hardships never come, he shouted, "Then what is the point of knowing God?"

Have you ever felt this way? You have tried to be a good Christian, and heartache still found you. Please know this: God gives us wisdom to avoid some of the hardships of life, but difficult seasons come to Christians and non-Christians alike. The difference is that Christians have God to comfort and sustain us in those times. Moreover, because of Christ, however long our troubles persist, eternity will swallow them one day. Praise God that He made a way for us to persevere through this life and to have joy in the next. The person who has never come to know

Christ will suffer trouble in this life without God's presence and then suffer eternal condemnation in the next. Christians win now and later. That is the point. That is our confident hope.

Whatever Is True

A PERFECT GUIDE

Thy word is truth.

— JOHN 17:17

I once followed the directions on my GPS, which took me to the wrong place. I followed the advice of someone I thought knew best. Their advice was faulty. Not so with the Word of God. People like to argue that the Bible is a book of fairy tales made up by man, but a look at what it says about itself shows otherwise. The

Bible says it is God-breathed (2 Timothy 3:16). It also says it is not any man's interpretation of the truth but that men were moved along by the Holy Spirit to write it (2 Peter 1:20-21). A God Who can create and sustain the world can also move men to write His Word without error. Such a God also can preserve it from corruption. Jesus Himself said that God's Word is truth.

The Scriptures require the Decoder called the Spirit of God to understand it.

The Word of God corrects when we are wrong, comforts us when we grieve, instructs when we are ignorant, and guides us with divine wisdom. A perfect guide can only come from a perfect God. Even better, that perfect God loves us enough to reveal Himself and communicate with us.

You may never understand everything you read in the Bible, my friend, but if you continue in it, the Word will read you. God has provided reliable teachers and preachers to help you understand His Word. Ask God to lead you to them. People have risked their lives to get a few pages of the Word. If you have a copy, appreciate it, read it, study it, and most of all, obey it because it is the perfect guide.

What adjustments must you make to spend more time reading God's roadmap?

Whatever Is Noble

DAY 40
THE LORD ALMIGHTY

*He who forms the mountains, who creates the
wind, and who reveals his thoughts to
mankind, who turns dawn to darkness, and
treads on the heights of the earth—the Lord
God Almighty is his name.*

— AMOS 4:13

He is the Almighty. Let that sink in. Nothing and no one ranks higher than He! This thought strikes awe. Who else is more worthy of respect than He? Of all kings and governors, He always tops the list. It is appropriate to bow before the Almighty. Majesty and worship belong to Him.

We honor men for their outstanding achievements. How much more does the Lord God deserve honor, glory, and respect.? He is the Creator of the earth, of the galaxies, and the microworld. He knows all, is everywhere at once, and has all power. Praise is due Him even if

He never did another thing for us. He is worthy of reverence for Who He is, separate from all He has done.

This knowledge overwhelms the mind, and greater still when we realize He loves us. Power coupled with cruelty evokes terror and despair, but what joy to know that the One with the most power has a warm place in His heart for you, my friend. No wonder the psalmist said,

"The Lord is with me, I will not be afraid. What can mere mortals do to me?" (Psalm 118:6)

Too often, we look to God only for what we can get from Him. He offers a great deal to us, and we need every bit of it, but for today, focus only on Who He is. What words of worship do you want to offer Him right now?

"Who is this, the king of glory? The LORD Almighty—he is the King of glory." (Psalm 24:10)

Whatever Is Right

DAY 41

BEFRIEND THE LONELY

But pity anyone who falls and has no one to help them up.

— ECCLESIASTES 4:9-10

I will never forget when I burst into tears on the way home from school one beautiful day in tenth grade. The tears surprised me, and the sobbing was intense. I recall asking myself why in the world I was crying. It took a few minutes to discover the answer, but it came through clearly as if someone had spoken out loud, "I am lonely. I have no friends!" I had a friend who abandoned me because I began talking too much about my faith, which embarrassed her. My temperament was quiet and timid; consequently, making friends did not come easily. God, in His compassion and love, saw my tears, and not long afterward, a lady at my church invited me to join a group of Christian youth at a weekly discipleship training.

Those weekly meetings were like water in a desert. That one

invitation opened the way to making friends in the group and with people they knew.

Social media intensifies loneliness. There is no substitute for in-person contact. We were made for human connection, and many suffer for lack.

Do not underestimate the power of entering the world of a lonely person. Think, my friend, and pray. Is there someone you can say a friendly "hello" to and get to know? It may be awkward at first, but it will be worth it. Please do not assume someone else will do it. Jesus loved everyone and gave His time so no one in His path was lonely. Who is in your path? Who can you be like Jesus for today?

Loneliness is a powerful drain, but friendship fills up the soul. Someone needs your company!

Whatever Is Pure

GOD'S MOTIVES

*When tempted, no one should say, 'God is
tempting me.' For God cannot be tempted by
evil, nor does he tempt anyone.*

— JAMES 1:13-15

As a child, I was only sure of my parents' love for me when I got candy and ice cream. When they spanked me, I assumed they hated me. Now that I am older, I know better.

When life is hard, our emotions can accuse God of things that are not true. Some people have concluded that God is cruel because He did not do what they expected. Some are angry enough at God to declare Him non-existent. Others assume God is mad at them because of the way life is going. We must not view God through the lens of our circumstances. Instead, we must view God through His Word. It says that God is light, and no darkness dwells in Him (1 John:5). His motives are never evil because His very essence is love. If God had wanted to destroy us, He would not have bothered with the cross. We were already condemned because of our sin (John 3:18). The question is not why bad things happen but why anything good happens, considering our sinfulness against a holy God. God's Word warns that we will have trouble in this world

(John16:33). He also promises that He will never leave us to handle those troubles alone (Hebrews 13:5b). Whenever your troubles tempt you to believe God is up to no good, search the Scriptures for answers that counteract those lies. Do not wait until hard times come. Plant seeds of truth in your heart every season of life, and your faith will be strong enough to remind you that God's motivation is always for you and not against you.

Whatever Is Lovely

DAY 43

DO NOT GLOAT

*Do not gloat when your enemy falls; when they
stumble, do not let your heart rejoice.*

— PROVERBS 24:17

What kind of love is this? The type that is unhappy when its enemy falls is a mature love that only God can give. What is the mindset behind agape love? It wants people to thrive. It wants its enemies to stop being enemies because of the judgment they set themselves up for. Jesus asked the Father to forgive those who crucified Him because they did not know what they were doing. They did not realize how wicked they were. They were blind to their sin and had a self-centered and skewed worldview.

Notice that today's verse says we are not to let our hearts rejoice over their downfall. It implies that we can decide about what our heart does. This is hard if you forget God supplies the power to choose like that. There is nothing natural about this way of loving. It is the same love that is not jealous because it is not insecure. This divine sort of love does not take pleasure in evil but rejoices when truth wins. This love is hard to fake. It takes its eyes off its troubles and sees beyond what is said and why. Hurt people hurt other people. Lost people act that way because they do not have the Spirit of God inside and are on their way to eternal judgment unless they respond to the gospel. They will live without the loving guidance of the Scriptures and the fellowship of the Body of Christ.

Gloating at their downfall is short-sighted and petty, considering these truths.

May God grant us grace not to be gloaters but givers of the Good News to our enemies instead.

Whatever Is Right

DAY 44
SAY "NO"

*Whoever rebukes a person will in the end gain
favor rather than one who has a flattering
tongue.*

— PROVERBS 28:23

Sometimes, we Christians act as though "no" is a dirty word. Where did we get the idea that we have to say "yes" to every request? Sometimes, we feel guilty for saying "no," even if it is the right thing to do. People who have trouble saying "no" can become enablers who stand in the way of growth and independence for others.

They provide an escape for people who need to feel the consequences of poor decisions. They go into debt, rescuing people who are happy to burn through their resources without repayment or change in behavior. Enablers call it "love," but real love wants what is best for the other person. Sometimes, saying "no" is the most mature thing you could do. It means risking rejection and misunderstanding for the sake of helping someone grow up. Free yourself from burdens God never told you to carry, my friend. Just because you feel selfish for saying "no" does not mean you are. False guilt and insecurity are toxic cousins. Ask God for wisdom to recognize both.

How do you find the courage to say "no"? It starts with the fear of God. When you recognize that God is your Supreme Authority, you can say "no" out of respect for

His rule in your life. Talk to God, tell Him why you are afraid to say "no "to what you know would not please Him. This will be an exercise in humbling self-discovery and personal growth. You will discover insecurity lurking in your heart.

Ask the Lord to pull it out by the roots. He will guide you to know your identity is not tied to pleasing people.

Whatever Is Pure

DAY 45
BROKENNESS BRINGS GROWTH

*Create in me a pure heart, O God, and renew a
steadfast spirit within me.*

— PSALM 51:10

Only God can create a pure heart, which He does with love and tenderness. We should feel guilty when we sin because that is what we are. However, God does not want us to wallow in our guilt. He desires we confess it and ask for His cleansing right away. Sometimes, we hesitate to ask for His cleansing because we focus on how much we do not deserve it. We allow shame to keep us from the throne of grace when God calls us to run to it. We grow frustrated and maybe embarrassed that we are still struggling with the same sin after all this time. Know that

God knew it would take this long, and just because you keep failing does not mean you will continue doing so.

Brokenness is the growth path! Growth takes time, and you have hope if your heart is tender about your sin. Resist the urge to gloss over your sin as if it is insignificant. No sin is insignificant, but sometimes we treat it that way because we hate the discomfort of guilt. We are in too big of a hurry to feel better that we skip brokenness. Brokenness is not the same as groveling. Groveling focuses on self-pity, whereas brokenness takes responsibility for the wrongdoing. Brokenness gives sin its rightful name and does not make excuses. It is where healing can begin because we see how powerless we are to change without God's help. It is the place where we get tired enough to surrender. Creating a pure heart is God's work, but we must cooperate with His process. Renew your commitment to let Him do His best work in you.

Think on This

Character is
turning down
the perfect

opportunity to
take advantage
of someone.

Whatever Is Worthy of Praise

❧

DAY 46
USE YOUR GIFTS

Now to each one the manifestation of the Spirit is given for the common good.

— 1 CORINTHIANS 12:7

God created you as a unique person. When He saved you from eternal condemnation through Christ, He gave you at least one spiritual gift so that you can be a blessing to His people. When you exercise that gift, beautiful things happen. You become more like Jesus. Other Christians will confirm your giftedness. You also experience joy, and God receives glory when you operate your special gift. You are a gift when you use your gift.

Do you want to know the best way to know your gift? Get busy. Pick something to do and see if "only God" things happen. Ask God to show you what He created you to do.

When I teach, I experience God working through me, unlike any other way. I have tried some things and learned they were not what God gifted me to do. When I began to teach

Bible stories to children after a time of training, it was as if I was flying. I loved it so much, and the Holy Spirit gave me ways to communicate biblical truth that resonated with the children. Since then, I have learned that God uses the same gift differently. One day, my ravenous appetite for teaching children disappeared. I never dreamed of teaching anyone under twelve because the idea terrified me. One day, my desire to speak and teach adults became like a fire that made me beg God for opportunities. It is the same gift, but I now use it differently.

The same may be true for you.

What is your spiritual gift(s)? Are you using it to serve others as God intended?

How might God be changing the way you use them?

Whatever Is True

∼

DAY 47

GOD IS IN CONTROL

The LORD has established his throne in heaven,
and his kingdom rules over all.

— PSALM 103:19

The sovereignty of God means He is in control. He loves you, and you can rejoice no matter what. The power of God can be a soft pillow for your heart when life is hard. It is a place to lay down all your questions and trust Him when you do not understand.

Remember this when elections go the opposite of what you had hoped, God is in control. When senseless tragedies leave you disillusioned, know that God is in control.

Remind yourself of God's jurisdiction over everything when unexpected sorrow comes your way. When the evening news reports make you anxious, say to yourself, "God is in control." These are opportunities to grow in trust in Him.

Whatever chaos the world brings, know that God is not confused or unaware. He said life would be challenging and offered His strength and peace to get through it. Heaven is your guaranteed destination if you completely trust in Christ. It is well with your soul, my friend. This puts everything else in perspective.

Knowing that God is in control takes the sting out of death and infuses peace in the face of terror. It combs the tangles out of frustration. Knowing we would need it in this hard life, oh, how loving God is to provide His presence. How beautiful that He left us with the truth that He is in control.

In what area of life do you need to remember God is in control today? What have you released but slowly taken back? Is there anything you feel does not need to be released because you have control? No, God asks you to release that as well. Think on these things.

Whatever Is Admirable

DAY 48
BE ON TIME

But everything should be done in a fitting and orderly way.

— 1 CORINTHIANS 14:40

"You can't be there at 10 o'clock by leaving home at 10," my daddy said. He was talking about being on time.

How can you do a better job of arriving on time? How can you train your children to do the same? Plan ahead. Give yourself time to find that lost shoe or your keys before the search has a chance to eat into your drive time. Doing a generous calculation of how long it will take to travel to your destination is a must. Once you've done that, tell yourself what time this means you must leave the house. Keep that specific time in your head the whole while you are getting ready. I like to add extra time in case I get lost or a traffic issue happens. I found I tend to let my mind wander in rooms that lack a clock, so make sure to have a clock in every room to prevent dawdling. If you need to make a stop on the way, add more time than you think you need. This cuts down on anxiety when the line is long at the store.

Train your children to do as much ahead of time as possible. Create a story about a child who is late and ask them to name specific actions the character could have taken to prevent tardiness. Help them apply these habits to their own lives. This will serve them well all their lives.

Punctuality is a life skill we all need. It shows respect for others and prevents unnecessary stress. Planning ahead is thinking on a good thing because it honors the time of others so that they are not spending it waiting for us.

Whatever Is Right

DAY 49

ASK FOR HELP

*If either of them falls down, one can help the
other up. But pity anyone who falls and has
no one to help them up.*

— ECCLESIASTES 4:10

P ride says, "I do not need anyone's help." God created us as interdependent beings, not independent ones. He never intended any of us never to need anybody.

Only God Almighty is self-sufficient. He says in Psalm 50:12, "If I were hungry, I would not tell you, for the world is mine, and all that is in it." If the Lord intended us never to need anyone, He would not have given each of us a different spiritual gift. He would have gifted everyone the same. Self-sufficiency sometimes masks a fear that needing help is a weakness. It may also fear repayment will be a hassle or a never-ending obligation. Self-sufficiency seeks to insulate itself, but it is a lonely prison that may have comforts but lacks the blessings that others can bring. Have you considered that those who thrive on giving suffer if we never need or ask for anyone's help? A need can be a road to unexpected blessings for the giver and receiver.

Need involves more than food or money. God created you to need companionship, encouragement, and perspective. As a Christian, you are part of the family of God.

What you have is necessary for the family's health; likewise, what others bring is vital to you. Do away with the idea that asking for help means you have failed.

Asking for help is admitting that you are not God. People tend to swallow their need instead of their pride. The abundant life Jesus promised involves having the blessing of receiving love from others who meet your needs. Please do not deprive yourself or them. Ask for help.

Whatever Is Pure

DAY 50
LOVE FROM A PURE HEART

*The goal of this command is love, which comes
from a pure heart, a good conscience, and a
sincere faith.*

— 1 TIMOTHY 1:5

The apostle Paul wrote to Timothy, his young disciple, to provoke Him to protect the believers at Ephesus from false teachers. Then, in today's devotional verse, the apostle explained why he gave this instruction. He wanted those believers to have a love from a pure heart, a good conscience, and a sincere faith. How could false teaching prevent these three essential traits? Since God is the only Source of truth, any other source is not pure. False teachers have selfish motives despite their talk about loving God. Their agenda always invites people to believe differently from what the Lord says. They can sound convincing, and they ruin those who follow them.

A filthy cup can only provide dirty water. Clean the cup;

the clean water will stay pure and nourish the drinker. Our hearts are like a cup. If we want a pure heart, we must only take in biblical truth and not some poisonous imitation. Pay close attention to what teachers and preachers say. Exercise discernment and trust the

Holy Spirit to alert you when something seems wrong. Do not let mere eloquence and passion be the criteria for believing a preacher. Check everything with the

Word and pay attention to context. Context is what is going on in the passage.

False teachers like to cut a verse in the Bible and paste it to make it mean something God never intended.

If you want to love from a pure heart, you must keep out the contamination of false teaching. The rewards of a pure heart, a good conscience, and sincere faith are worth the effort. Think on this and grow!

Whatever Is Admirable

ᨠᨠᨠ

DAY 51

CHEERFULNESS

A happy heart makes the face cheerful, but
heartache crushes the spirit.

— PROVERBS 15:13

"What's wrong?" Everybody kept asking me this. I did not know the answer. Then, one day, I surprised myself because I burst into tears and did not know why. I had to work hard to stop sobbing and asked myself why I was crying. The answer surfaced, "I am lonely. I have no friends." Sometimes, our faces tell a story we do not know is being written. Other times, we may learn to hide what our hearts do not want anyone to know. Cheerfulness is the result of what our hearts tell us. Not long after the crying incident, God brought people into my life who loved me and accepted me as I was. I learned not to take myself so seriously, and best of all, I learned who I am in Christ. People who know me now talk about my smile. I rejoice to hear them talk about it because, for the longest time, I had a heaviness about me. My face changed when my thoughts changed.

No one is always jolly, but joy can be our face's overarching message. Jesus wants you to have complete joy, and it comes in His presence (Psalm 16:11). God is greater than any circumstance you face today, my friend. Meditate on all that is true about God and you because you belong to Him. It is okay to cry if you are hurting, but you must intentionally remind yourself what is truer than why you are crying. David learned to encourage himself in the Lord (1 Samuel 30:6) . You can, too. People who smile in difficulty see beyond circumstances to the truth. God has a reputation for faithfulness; therefore, you can have a good reputation for cheerfulness.

Whatever is Admirable

〰️

DAY 52
LOVE THEM IN THEIR WAY

Love one another.

— JOHN 13:34-35

One of my English Literature teachers in college once said, "If you want to show love to your children, find out what they want, then go out and get it for them!" She went on to tell of an object she bought for her young adult son and how she could not wait to see his eyes light up.

When you love someone, you want to express it. We often express it in the way we most enjoy receiving love. For example, if you most enjoy hearing someone say out loud that they love you, you are likely to express love by saying it to others. However, the one you love may most enjoy receiving gifts as an expression of love. If you only ever verbalize your love without tangible gifts, you miss an opportunity to bring special joy to your loved one.

We mean well, but we need God's help to show we care

intentionally. He knows how He has wired the people you love. Ask Him for insight into how to make them feel appreciated and loved. God loves to be involved in every part of your life. Also, listen with great attention to what your loved one says. They can give clues to what is important to them without realizing it. If you are not sure what to do, ask them. Communication is one of the most loving actions you can take to enrich every relationship. It says you care enough to ask and listen to what is important to them. It says you want to try to love them their way, not yours. Of course, we never express love in a way that violates God's commands.

Who will you show love to today? How will you choose to express it?

Whatever Is True

DAY 53
YOU NEED IT

Two are better than one...but pity the one who has no one to lift him up.

— ECCLESIASTES 4:9-10

You will never grow as strong attending regular worship services as in a small group. God never intended you to isolate yourself to the point you have no accountability or accessibility to other believers intimately. Being vulnerable about your struggles is frightening, but so is being alone in your trials. You need other believers to encourage you and come alongside you in your struggles. You need to know you are not alone. When you connect with growing believers, you will discover you are not as different as you may think.

Good times are better with people who love you. Bad times are easier, too.

How can anyone grow to love you if you are never around long enough to connect? Relationships take time and proximity to build. What are you doing to ensure this happens? The devil loves it when Christians keep to themselves. He convinces them they can grow just fine with their Bible and Jesus alone. He wants them to forget that community among believers was so important to Jesus that

He prayed for it before He went to the cross (John 17:20). Satan dupes Christians into trying to handle life alone so that when life overwhelms them, they are without the kind of help that comes because deep relationships have been built beforehand.

If a community has hurt you, ask God to lead you to another one. You will never find a perfect group, but you cannot afford to live without a healthy group of believers. God has called you to do great things, but He has not called you to do it alone. You need fellow believers, and they need you. Think on these things.

Whatever Is Noble

DAY 54
HONESTY

*The Lord detests dishonest scales, but accurate
weights find favor with him.*

— PROVERBS 11:1

I had a lot on my mind that day. Because my husband had received a serious health diagnosis the day before, grocery shopping had been a stressful activity. I remember getting a headache due to overthinking because I did not know what foods to buy and not to buy. Loading the car and driving home, I realized too late that I had left my purse in the basket in the parking lot. I went back, and the store manager said an employee had found the purse. All the cash we had to live on for the rest of that week was missing. With no way to trace who had taken the money,

I had to accept that I would never see it again.

Isn't it a shame that honesty is hard to find? The last time I thought I had dropped some money at a gas station, I did not bother to return because of the unlikeliness that someone would turn it in.

Honesty is important to the Lord, and those who bear the name of Christ should be known for their integrity. People in the world steal because they do not fear God.

They either believe there is no God to Whom they are accountable, or they lack the faith to acquire what they need in God's way. Why do Christians steal? Why do they lie on their tax forms?

Because honesty is hard to find, it is worthy of honor whenever we see it. Honesty has a perspective that most people do not have. It recognizes that acquiring anything the wrong way may yield an instant result, but it also carries a built-in consequence. Nothing escapes the Lord's notice.

Whatever Is Right

DAY 55
FORGIVE OTHERS

*Bear with each other and forgive one another if
any of you has a grievance against someone.
Forgive as the Lord forgave you.*

— COLOSSIANS 3:13

For the child of God, forgiving others is not optional. It is a by-product of Christian love, which is how you can know you belong to Jesus. Forgiving does not mean offenders get away with anything; it means you leave payback to God.

How can we be unforgiving when God has forgiven us so much? We may not have done what others have done to us, but we have offended a perfect and holy God.

His forgiveness is our pattern: we are to forgive the way He forgave us. How did

He forgive us? He forgave by grace. This means we did not deserve the forgiveness He gave. God forgave us because of Who He is, not because of who we are. Forgive those who hurt you because God forgave you when you did not deserve it. Forgiveness has nothing to do with deserving.

God forgave fully. He did not pick which sins to forgive but forgave them all.

Some sins are more challenging for us to forgive than others, but we are called to be as thorough in our forgiveness of others as God is of us.

Forgiveness does not mean you must let your offender back into your life. Some fear forgiving because they worry that this obligates them to let their offender back into their life. God never leaves us, but He is God and promised never to end His relationship with His children. You are not God, and ending a relationship is within your basket of choices to make about your offenders. Sometimes, this is a necessary consequence of human relationships. God enforces consequences even as He forgives. Think on this!

Whatever Is Pure

DAY 56
KEEP GOOD COMPANY

One who loves a pure heart and who speaks with grace will have the king for a friend.

— PROVERBS 22:11

King Solomon is the author of this verse. What kind of person does he say he wants to have around him? He wants a person who loves a pure heart. Do you know people who only associate with bad company? What have you noticed about them? Do they tend to be negative most of the time? Does gossip make up most of what they talk about? What influence would these people have on you if you spent much time with them? King Solomon had a nation to run and knew he did not have time to mix with anyone who might taint his thinking. You may not be king of a country, but you have an assignment from God at your job, home, and church.

Never underestimate the power people you hang around will have on how you present yourself in your circles of influence. Choosing wise and graceful friends is a spiritual exercise.

The king also desired to have friends who spoke with grace. This is important because what emerges from a person's mouth reveals what is in her heart. A young woman saw me in distress one day. She asked what was wrong, and I knew not to share anything. I had seen the way she and her friends talked about people. I knew she would take everything I told her back to her posse. I also noticed the little critical remarks she made whenever she disliked how I expressed my individuality.

Listen to words people say; they are a window into their hearts.

What kind of people do you want as friends? Might God be calling you to distance yourself from someone hindering your growth?

Whatever is Lovely

DAY 57
NO GOSSIPING

*The words of a gossip are like choice morsels; they
go down to the inmost parts.*

— PROVERBS 18:8

A juicy embarrassment happened to a young woman, and everyone was whispering. A person in charge of handling the situation was approached by someone who pretended to want to help. I recall the leader saw straight through to the motives of the overeager volunteer who only wanted to get close enough to dredge up more ugly details to broadcast.

Gossip is hard to resist. For some reason, hearing about embarrassing things happening to others feels good. It may make us feel better about ourselves. We may find it entertaining to hear bad things on television happen to someone we know. Why do we enjoy sharing this kind of news with others? Christlike love desires to protect others (1 Corinthians 13:7). It does not delight in the downfall of another. It is not eager to share information it would not want to be shared if things were reversed. Gossip is like tasty morsels, but Christian love can curb your appetite for it.

Gossip sometimes reveals insecurity in the one doing it. It may also reflect anger or jealousy because gossip derives pleasure from harming the reputation of someone people look up to. Gossip rejoices when private faults are on public display. Jesus would never do any of these things, would He?

If you struggle with gossip, remember that you will give an account to God for every word. Gossip is the fruit of a rotten root. Ask God to reveal the core of why you gossip. He is loving enough to show you so that you can find healing. He can make you like water that stops the fires of gossip instead of gasoline that spreads it. Think on these things.

Whatever Is Admirable

DAY 58
WHILE THERE IS STILL TIME

*Therefore, as we have opportunity, let us do good
to everyone, especially to the family of faith.*

— GALATIANS 6:10

While there is time, tell someone you love them. They will never get tired of hearing it. Thank your parents for everything they did right and forgive them for their mistakes. Apologize to that person you hurt. Do not worry about how they might respond; you will be lighter.

Visit someone lonely. Make an extra pot of soup while making your own and share it with an exhausted young mother. Make memories with the young people in your life. Long after you are gone, they will cherish them.

At this writing, three mass shootings occurred in my country in a week. You or I could have been victims in any of those places. Those families thought they had more time with their loved ones. So did the victims. Life is uncertain; therefore, we are wise to make the most of every opportunity to do good and make a difference. You and I have no control over when our lives will end, but we can control what we do with today. What phone call do you need to make? What text do you need to send? Is there a check you have meant to write to encourage someone in need? Make today a day of adding as many good things as possible to the list of ways you are a blessing. If today was your last day on earth, would you be satisfied with the last thing you said to people in your life? Who needs to hear you share the gospel with them? Souls hang in the balance, my friend.

All you have is today. Make it count while there is still time. Think on these things.

Whatever Is Admirable

∽

DAY 59

GOODNESS

But the fruit of the Spirit is ... goodness.

— GALATIANS 5:22

Goodness may be hard to define, but you know it when you see it. The Holy Spirit produces it in the believer, and blessed are those receiving it. When you have a need, and someone supplies it and throws in something extra, you have experienced goodness.

Do you know people who have a reputation for being good to people? An older saint who has now gone to heaven exemplified this quality. He had a reputation for being good to everyone in any way he could. Fearless in his generosity, he never made you feel inferior or like it inconvenienced him to give. He seemed always to be searching for ways to be good to you. It sounds a lot like Jesus, does it not?

Think about ways others have shown you goodness. How did it make you feel?

How often do you exercise goodness to your neighbors and

friends? Be careful that your goodness is not limited to those outside your home. Remember to be good to your husband, children, and parents. Be intentional about saying a good word, doing a good deed, and ensuring you do not take anyone for granted.

The world expects us Christians to be harsh and judgmental. Sometimes, this is because they do not like God's truth we tell them, but sometimes they are right.

Sometimes, Christians forget they are sinners and still have work to do on themselves. Like steak served with spinach, goodness is an excellent accompaniment to speaking the hard truth to people. Goodness softens the heart and opens the ears. Determine that whatever else people may say about you, they cannot deny your goodness to them.

Whatever Is Worthy of Praise

❧

DAY 60

SUBMISSION

*In your relationships with one another, have the
same mindset as Christ Jesus.*

— PHILIPPIANS 2:5

Our sinful nature makes us always desire to be first,
but healthy relationships require mutual submission. Our society sees submission as demeaning, but
when it is practiced for the good of others, it is beautiful.
Abusers use submission as a weapon, but this was never God's
intention. Submission ensures everyone, not just one person,
gets their needs and desires met. No one should always win at
the expense of others. Every person is important in submission.
It helps the giver receive the blessing that only giving renders
(Acts 20:35). For the receiver, worth and value are instilled, as
well as an opportunity to experience love from others.

Selfishness short-circuits both.

We teach our children to take turns. This involves submitting the desire to have the toy first so the other child can enjoy it. We submit to traffic laws for the safety of others on the road. We submit to our husbands to maintain order and to flourish in our essential role as women. Fear makes submission suspect, but the Holy Spirit makes it valuable. Anyone who submits to another gains favor from God and imitates Jesus.

We do not have to have the last word in every debate with a spouse or friend.

Sometimes, letting the other person have their way is wise and right. Fear says they may always want it if you let them have their way. The truth is that healthy boundaries will keep that fear from becoming reality.

Sometimes, we submit to others out of love for them. Other times, submission is an act of love for God, trusting that He will reward you in due time for your deference.

How is God calling you to submit today?

Whatever Is True

∞

GOD IS YOUR PROVIDER

And my God will meet all your needs...

— PHILIPPIANS 4:19

George Muller was a man of great faith, and after reading His biography, I wanted to be like him. Mueller was a man of prayer who started and maintained multiple orphanages in England and never asked anyone for money to run them. He only prayed and, time after time, God provided. When I finished the biography, God called me to go back to school. I did not know how I would pay for it, so I asked the Lord if I could trust Him to provide for me the way He had for George Muller.

I was not to take out any loans but to trust Him to provide for my education. For seven years, the Lord did amazing things to provide. I cannot say I was always full of faith, but God was always faithful.

God has promised to provide all your needs. He is Jehovah-Jireh, and He knows what you need before you ask. He always provides for what is His will. Think of how you love to provide for your children. God loves providing for you even more.

A good father always provides for his children, and God is that Good Father to you!

He has not promised to provide all you want but all you need. He is good about providing some of your wants too. He has not promised to supply your needs in the way you want, but He will provide in His way. He knows what is best. Anyone who trusts God to provide will grow for sure!

Those years of tuition provision taught me much about myself and God. The same will be true for you. What do you need to trust God to provide for you today?

Whatever Is Right

DAY 62

GOOD STEWARDSHIP

*Now, it is required that those who have been
given a trust must prove faithful.*

— 1 CORINTHIANS 4:2

Everything you have is a gift from God. The money you make by working is a gift because God gave you the strength to earn it. The children you are raising are His gifts, too. The time you get with each new day is a gift more precious than money because you can only spend it once. If your health is good, God graced you with it.

He wants you and I to be good stewards of what He gives. A steward is a manager in charge of what belongs to someone else. How would you spend your money differently if you remembered all you have belongs to God? What about your time? Please understand that it is not a sin to spend some of your time in rest. Rest is a gift, too.

Your relationship with God is more than a servant-Master relationship. He is not standing over you, scowling at every little thing. It is also a Father-child relationship full of love and grace. Do you spend time talking to Him throughout each day? Can you think of an area of your life that your heavenly Father wants to empower you to manage better? Ask Him to search your heart to reveal any activity He wants you to stop because it wastes His gifts. Perfection is not your goal; faithfulness is. Be faithful to train your children to live for Jesus. Be faithful to give to the Lord's work. Be faithful to steward your time so that it is not always about you but is also spent serving others. Every good gift comes from God. Be thankful for each of them and use them for the glory of God.

Whatever Is Pure

DAY 63

FEAR OF GOD

The fear of the Lord is pure, enduring forever.

— PSALM 19:9

The psalm-writer is gushing about the Word of God in Psalm 19:7-10. He declares that the Word of God is perfect and restores the soul. He states that what God says is sure, and it imparts wisdom. He further praises the Word as right and how it gladdens the heart. The cadence continues as the writer says that the Word gives insight because it is pure. Then, like a driver who hits the brakes without warning,

David inserts a statement about the fear of the Lord. Why does he insert this ruby in the middle of a parade of diamonds? How can the fear of the Lord be pure, and how does it endure forever?

To fear God is to honor and respect Him. The World sees respect for God as

foolish. They say we do it out of terror or ignorance, not because He is real or loving. The fool says there is no God, but

139

this is the height of disrespect. Fearing the Lord acknowledges His existence. This respect will go on forever because there will never be a time when God ceases to exist. Enduring respect is only suitable for an eternal God. Also, the everlasting God will forever be worthy of respect because

His flawless character never changes. I guess talking about the Word sparked a logical leap to talking about the God Who wrote it. How can anyone think about

His pure Word without thinking about its divine Author? How can we think about the Author without worship and honor?

Today, honor the Lord in how you use His name and treat His children. Fear Him by your obedience. Fearing Him is a pure and eternal activity that starts now.

Whatever Is Admirable

DAY 64

MODESTY

I also want the women to dress modestly, with decency and propriety, adorning themselves, not with elaborate hairstyles or gold or pearls or expensive clothes.

— 1 TIMOTHY 2:9

Today's verse speaks about modesty. I knew a girl who often wore flashy, tight clothes with plunging necklines and as little fabric as possible. She was beautiful and did not need to dress this way, but she did not seem to know it. Proverbs 11:22 says, "Like a gold ring in a pig's snout is a beautiful woman who shows no discretion." Discretion considers other people. Wearing clothes that draw attention to private parts disrespects men and their wives. It draws the wrong kind of attention. Immodest dress is often a mark of insecurity. "Notice me! I do not care what it takes," is the desperate message that dressing this way sends. We who know Christ must recognize that our value is not in our physical beauty but in who we are in Christ. The world teaches women to use their sexuality to get what they want, but a child of God knows she never needs to sacrifice her dignity to get anything her heavenly Father has promised for the asking.

Be careful not to go to extremes. Some would interpret today's verse to mean a woman must never look beautiful. They may accuse the apostle Paul of belittling women and encouraging them to be frumpy and wear nothing that enhances their beauty. That would be going to extremes to avoid the real message of this verse.

God made you beautiful, and anyone with eyes can see it. A confident woman dresses modestly and accentuates the positive features God gave her without harming any man's imagination or demeaning herself by revealing too much. Do you have a good reputation for dressing modestly?

Whatever Is True

DAY 66
STAY CLOSE TO BEAR FRUIT

No branch can bear fruit by itself; it must
remain in the vine.

— JOHN 15:4

Abiding in Christ is the only hope you and I have of accomplishing anything worthwhile. Just as you could not save yourself, you cannot live the Christian life in your power. Jesus illustrated how to live for Him using the vine and the branches. Jesus said He is the True Vine, and we Christians are branches. Just as the branch on any plant must stay connected to the vine, so must we abide in (remain connected to) Christ so that He can bear fruit through us. It is not the job of the branch to bear fruit. Staying connected to the vine is the branch's job, and fruit-bearing will happen because it does it through the vine.

What does it mean to abide or to remain in Christ? Abiding is intimacy and relationship with Jesus, not just belonging to Him. You can be a child of God through salvation but not enjoy the relationship abiding in Christ brings. If you are not abiding, you are not growing.

How do you abide in Christ so that you bear much fruit? Obedience is a sure way to yield fruit. What is God commanding you to do today that you have yet to obey? Obeying God means you will bear fruit because you will go in the same direction and let Him use you to accomplish His will. Serving and having a humble attitude also promote growth. Who needs what you have that you can share with today? Associate with people unlike you the way Jesus did, and you will produce fruit that will never perish. Stay close to God today, follow His leading, and you will be a branch laden with spiritual fruit!

Whatever Is Right

DAY 67

BE SHREWD AND INNOCENT

I am sending you out like sheep among wolves.
Therefore, be as shrewd as snakes and as
innocent as doves.

— MATTHEW 10:16

Some think that to be a Christian, you must be stupid and naïve. They say Christianity is irrelevant because living as the Bible says in today's cutthroat world is impossible. Do you think Jesus was aware of the world you and I live in when He called us to be shrewd and innocent? Of course, He was! That is why He said He sends us out like sheep among wolves. A sheep is vulnerable. Refusing to join in when everyone else is cheating makes you susceptible to ridicule. It is a challenge to tell the truth when lying is easier. That does not mean it is okay to cheat or lie to fit in. It does mean you must rely on God's strength to remain faithful. You are to remain innocent of wrongdoing even if you must stand alone.

The world champions self-reliance at the expense of everything else, but God champions faithfulness to Him.

What does it mean to be shrewd as a snake? It means you must act with wisdom.

For example, if you do not want to tell the boss you saw your coworkers stealing, you are wise to stay away when they are doing it. God calls you to shine like light, but it does not mean you go looking for trouble. When trouble finds you, stand firm.

Remember that His glory and your growth are God's main objectives, not your comfort. God receives glory if you stand firm when it is unpopular. When you choose to lose, you will point people to Christ if winning means you must cheat.

Be innocent. Be shrewd. Think on these things.

Whatever Is Pure

DAY 68

WHAT YOU SAY

The Lord detests the thoughts of the wicked, but
gracious words are pure in His sight.

— PROVERBS 15:26

I had a friend who loved to say ugly words. She loved bantering with hurtful verbal assaults and always said she was only teasing. I did not remain friends with her for long.

Some Christians use profanity at home but clean their language up at church. If love is to be the banner for the Christian, our words matter. Just because someone laughs at the insults you hurl at them does not mean they like it. Our words have incredible power. They can tear someone down and make them lose confidence. Our words can also encourage, empower, and lighten a load. The words we say are like a recording that our listeners repeatedly hear. What kind of recording are you making in the minds of those around you?

Some parents believe that harsh words toughen a child and

prepare them for the world. Nowhere in Scripture does God encourage cruel words for building up a person's spirit. Proverbs 15:1 warns that harsh words stir up anger while soft ones keep anger away. The apostle Paul encouraged Christian fathers not to exasperate their children (Ephesians 6:4).

Encouraging words increase productivity in employees. A spouse who praises her mate will reap a harvest of gratitude. It is human nature to rise to the level of the compliments made to us.

Will you purpose to share at least one encouraging word for every person you encounter today? Even those who are grouchy need to know someone cares. Why not offer to pray for what bothers them?

This day is ripe with opportunities to use your words to make a difference. Make

God proud by reflecting His grace through your words today.

Whatever Is Worthy of Praise

⟨∿⟩

DAY 69

BE THAT ONE

So that you may become blameless and pure, children of God without fault in a warped and crooked generation. Then you will shine among them like stars in the sky.

— PHILIPPIANS 2:15

There was a hallway I dreaded walking down because I never knew what kind of mood the workers would be in on any given day. People in that hallway had an air of superiority, making me nervous. One woman, however, always had a Christ-like disposition, a smile, and a way of making you feel worthy of respect. Are you that person at your job? Are you the one people feel at ease with? Do they think their secrets are safe with you? Treat people the way Jesus would. Refuse to talk about another employee behind their back unless you are bragging about them.

What if you have already been the opposite of all those things? What if you have been less like Jesus already? I knew a lady who decided she was not going to like me. She initially assumed the worst about me and was snippy when talking to me.

She called me to her office one day, and my stomach was in knots. I tried to think of what I did wrong that she wanted to criticize. Imagine my shock when she had kind words for me, a smile, and a compliment. It was like meeting Scrooge on

Christmas morning! At first, I was not sure if she was faking or not. Over time, she proved to be genuine. I do not know what made her change, but I share this story because if she can change, you can too!

Your circle of influence needs someone to show Jesus makes a difference. Be that one. The Holy Spirit will empower you, and you will grow!

Whatever Is Honorable

DAY 70
RICHNESS OF REPETITION

*It is no trouble for me to write the same things to
you again, and it is a safeguard for you.*

— PHILIPPIANS 3:1

Has your pastor or teacher ever invited you to turn to a passage so familiar that you groaned inwardly *"Not this again!?"* Were you tempted to tune out the rest of the teaching time? We may think we have studied that subject, or passage so often that we don't need to hear it again. If we have been believers for a long time and studied

Scripture for many years, we may miss what God wants to say to us. Repetition has excellent value in Bible study, my friend. First, we are more prone to forget than we realize. Thank repetition for your familiarity. Embrace repetitions to retain that familiarity. Second, we may have heard those verses before, but we need to see them in light of our present season. Be encouraged to humbly ask what the Lord wants to say or remind you of this time.

Third, false teachers are so cunning that if we are not discerning, they can deceive us by altering just one word. Repetition conditions us to see through subtle lies.

Fourth, sometimes, we think we need a new word from God when the old one is sufficient. Scripture is like the ocean; it always holds the same amount of content, but its depths are inexhaustible. Ask God to help you to see the same truths with fresh eyes.

Use the opportunity to bask anew in old truth.

Finally, familiarity is not the same as mastery. We all know more than we have obeyed. Repetition may be God's way of inviting you to live what you learn in more areas.

Repetition is rich with opportunities for growth.

Whatever Is Admirable

DAY 71
IF IT WOULD NOT LOOK RIGHT...

Abstain from all appearance of evil.

— 1 THESSALONIANS 5:22

Sometimes, an innocent act looks like it is anything but that. You have a spiritual enemy who is always looking for a way to destroy you and your witness for Christ (John 10:10). You are wise to do everything in your power to frustrate his efforts by avoiding any situation or practice that could have the appearance of wrongdoing.

Present receipts when dealing with other people's money. Never let yourself be alone too long with someone of the opposite sex. You may not be doing anything wrong, but do not give suspicious minds the chance to make something up. Do not underestimate the devil's inability to resist an opportunity to ruin your reputation or ministry. You do not have to be paranoid, but be wise, my friend.

Maybe you have a heart of gold and tend to express care with a lot of physical touch. Please exercise wisdom as to when this could be misinterpreted. When caring for young children who are not your own, be wise when helping them in the bathroom. It is sad that we must be so cautious, but this is the world we live in, and ignoring this can make you sorry you did. It is better to be safe than to live with regret and scandal. As a child of God, do all you can to protect your witness. Be sensitive to what the Holy Spirit says in these situations. If something might not look right, do your part to ensure it does not look wrong.

Decide beforehand what parameters will be your habit. Stick to them even though others may think you are legalistic or overly cautious. The enemy often accuses us when we are the most careless. Think on these things.

Whatever Is Admirable

DAY 72
MEEKNESS

Blessed are the meek.

— MATTHEW 5:5

The best example I have witnessed of meekness occurred in a seminary class. A professor who held a controversial view on a particular subject invited students to ask questions. One student came close to insulting the professor, and for the briefest moment, I saw anger flicker in the teacher's eyes. Had I blinked, I would have missed it. The teacher then shifted his weight to the other foot, cleared his throat, and smiled. His words were gentle and kind, although he had the power and knowledge to lambast the young student to embarrassment.

Meekness is a reputable quality that is hard to find. Anger is more effortless than controlling oneself. Retaliating can earn an enviable reputation for being tough.

Meekness can look like weakness, although it takes great strength to exercise it.

Meekness has a confidence that does not need to prove its worth. It springs from the truth that only Jesus gets to define your identity. You do not need to show off because you know that pride is a sin. If you want to be meek, imitate Jesus. He said, "Take my yoke upon you and learn from me, for I am gentle and humble in heart, and you will find rest for your souls." That means to concern yourself with what is important to Him. Anger, self-righteousness, and rashness are burdensome and exhausting. When you walk in step with Christ, you find rest because He is bearing the load, not you. Ask Him to turn your eyes away from caring what other people think. He will give you a mind that focuses on Him and His agenda. It is the path to peace and joy.

Prayer: Father, I want to be meek like your Son. Change my focus. Renew my mind. Amen.

Whatever Is Worthy of Praise

❧

DAY 73
YOUR STORY IS NOT OVER YET

*Let us not become weary in doing good, for at the
proper time, we will reap a harvest if we do
not give up.*

— GALATIANS 6:9

Have you been trying to do the right thing for a long while, but it seems to be doing no good? Maybe you have failed recently and feel discouraged and disappointed in yourself. You wonder if staying down wouldn't be easier instead of risking getting knocked down if you get back up. This life is harder than you imagined, and you don't know how much more you can take.

Let me offer you an encouraging perspective, my friend. Every winner has been where you are now. This is just the dark part of your story, and you need to stick around for the brighter part. Do not doubt; do not give up. Cry if you must but keep moving. "Weeping may endure for a night, but joy comes in the morning" (Psalm 30:5).

Keep doing what you know is right and ask God what to do afterward. You can't fail when you keep following God's instructions. Recognize that He does not work on our timetable but is fully aware of how you feel. If you have run out of strength, God offers His.

You may not know what to do, but you do know that giving up before God steps in is not the answer. Let Him hold you while you struggle. Let Him dry your tears; He collects them in a bottle, you know. Cling to His promises in this dark place.

Hold out until you see the next step, my friend. God is up to something good in your life, and you are going to be soul-deep glad you stayed around to see it.

Whatever Is Worthy of Praise

◦◦◦

DAY 74
BROTHERLY LOVE

*Therefore, as we have opportunity, let us do good
to all people, especially to those who belong to
the family of believers.*

— GALATIANS 6:10

When we come to Christ for salvation, we inherit a new family. All who share in redemption through repentance and faith are brothers and sisters in Christ. The "one another's" in Scripture has other Christians as target recipients. Their needs become your concern, their burdens are yours to share, and vice-versa. We should not neglect blood relatives, but other Christians get special attention.

This can be lost in a local fellowship of believers if we do not intentionally see each other as family. It is the most beautiful sight to observe Christians caring for one another. The watching world noted how Christians loved each other in the early Church. They shared with anyone among them who had a need and stood with each other in the face of persecution. When we realize we are one in Christ, it will dramatically affect how we treat each other.

You don't have to know them to show love to them. A Christian on the other side of the world is your sister or brother; you can send help without knowing them.

In the olden days, a person traveling to a new town had to have a letter of reference to receive favor in the community. Nobody would hire them if they didn't know them or have a mutual friend. The Holy Spirit is all the reference you need in the Body of Christ. If they belong to Christ, they belong to you. You belong to them.

God is worthy of praise because He gave us each other. We are all different, but essential.

Whatever is Admirable

∽

DAY 75

MAD AT GOD?

*Simon Peter answered him, 'Lord, to whom shall
we go? You have the words of eternal life.*

— JOHN 6:68

Jesus had just shared some words that were hard to
swallow, and many of His followers left Him. He then
turned to the twelve who were left and asked if they
wanted to abandon Him, too. Peter's response was bril-
liant. He answered Jesus' question with a question: Where else
could they go since Jesus had the words of eternal life? There
are no substitutions for what Jesus offers, my friend.

Sometimes, He allows, does, or commands things that
anger us. We may be tempted to look elsewhere, but that is a
futile use of energy. NOBODY can comfort, save, heal, counsel,
provide, or love like He does.

What are we to do if leaving Him is not the best option?
God is not shocked or afraid of your anger. He knows that we
only have part of the picture and that our anger is not based on

all the facts. Times like these are rich with growth opportunities. We can pause and remember Who we are dealing with: Almighty God. He never failed in anything He promised, so we are wise to wait for the deliverance we are impatient to receive. Remember that God knows what He is doing, and you can trust Him. Itemize all the times you thought He forgot you but later learned He was up to something good. This time is no different.

Instead of walking away from God, talk to Him. Share your anger with reverent honesty. Ask Him to give you His perspective. Also, journal your thoughts to revisit the pit you thought would swallow you and rejoice when you see what God was up to all along. Think on these things.

Whatever Is Worthy of Praise

༄

DAY 76
NO CONDEMNATION

*Therefore, there is now no condemnation for
those who are in Christ Jesus.*

— ROMANS 8:1

Have you noticed the word "now" in today's verse? It implies that there was a time when there was condemnation for us. We stood condemned because we could not keep God's laws perfectly. We were the Walking Dead, born with a sinful nature woven into our spiritual DNA. God did not want us to remain this way, and we could do nothing to help ourselves.

In His great mercy, He made a way to honor His law that sin must be punished and simultaneously set us free from the condemnation He had every right to exercise.

He sent His Son, the only Candidate for the job, to die for something He didn't do to save those who did everything they shouldn't. Entering the world in the vulnerable form of a Child, He escaped death many times until God said it was time to die. He effortlessly checked all the boxes prophecy said would identify Him.

Then came the time to die. He felt all the things any human would feel at such a time, yet His will to obey the Father overrode His natural desire to dodge the horrors of the cross. Three days later, He escaped a sealed tomb, peeling off death like a robe and making cameo appearances to the disciples. Finally, like a superhero, He ascended before their eyes, promising to return the same way. When

He got back home, He sat down at the Father's right hand and now watches with joy as many receive His gift—all of this He did to rid us of condemnation. There is now none! For this, He is indeed worthy of praise!

Whatever Is Right

DAY 77

PUT UP A FIGHT!

Hate what is evil....

— ROMANS 12:9

C hristians are taught to love, but there is also a time to hate. Hate what is evil and resist it because it stands against everything God loves. Exploitation, corruption, heresy, inequality, and intimidation are only a few evils plaguing our world. Evil is like a fire that will consume anything unless something or someone thwarts it. Evil is invisible, but you can see its effect everywhere. It can be overwhelming and frightening, but you are neither helpless nor hopeless, my friend. As a child of

God, you have tremendous power to stand against evil and make a difference. Evil loves silence, so be determined to speak up. Evil loves cowardice, so you must be brave. Evil asks, "Who do you think you are?" You must answer, "I am more than an overcomer through Christ" (Romans 8:37). Evil wins when you run away, so you must stand (Ephesians 6:11). Determine that with God's help, evil will have to step back because you are not going anywhere. Are you not tired of the devil devouring your family, friends, government, and community? It is not an easy fight, but you have already won because the One Who lives in you is greater than the evil one who is in the world (1 John 4:4). It is right to resist evil because there is too much at stake if you do not. The vulnerable, weak, poor, and mistreated cannot fight for themselves. It is right for you to be a part of the solution. You cannot do everything for everyone, but you can do something. What is one way you can resist evil today? If you do not know, ask God. He will show you and empower you. Evil has reigned long enough!

Whatever Is Admirable

❦

DAY 78

BE BLAMELESS

... so that you may become blameless and pure,
children of God without fault in a warped
and crooked generation. Then you will shine
among them like stars in the sky.

— PHILIPPIANS 2:15

erfection is impossible, but you can be blameless. We who love Jesus want to be the best example for His glory, but we fall short. We ask His forgiveness when we fail, and He promised to cleanse us of our guilt. What about the people you fail?

What do you do when you respond incorrectly or say something you regret? If you want to be blameless, humility is what you need. Apologize and make restitution if you can. People may surprise you when you humble yourself. They already know you are not perfect, but when you ask their forgiveness, you become blameless in their eyes. An apology says you value how you present yourself as a Christian. It makes it harder for them to say your relationship with Christ is not real and points them to God. That is what you want more than anything. People sometimes fear embracing Christianity because the standard is so high, and they know they cannot live up to it. When they see you admit your failure, it shows the grace of God. Who says this will not cause them to consider a relationship with Christ, too?

Also, if you have received Christ's salvation, you look blameless to God (Colossians 1:22). Your guilt and shame are cleansed because you are hidden under the blood of Christ. Rejoice in this truth today, my friend. Let your gratitude to God propel you to extend the same grace to others. Let it also help you forgive yourself, which can sometimes be the hardest to do.

Prayer: Lord, help me to live a blameless life. Amen

Whatever Is Admirable

DAY 79
OBEY WHEN IT IS UNPOPULAR

We must obey God rather than human beings.

— ACTS 5:29

People will not always understand your faith. The Bible warns that unbelievers can't understand because they do not have the Spirit of God (1 Corinthians 2:14).

You operate from a different standard than the world. Ask God for the courage to focus on the His will above everything else.

When my husband and I decided to educate our children at home, many well-meaning people did not understand. They raised concerns about our children having enough friends their age and being able to communicate well. None of those were ever an issue with our children. People would quiz them on specific subjects to see if they needed to improve. They never were. I understood their concerns, but they were unnecessary. We followed our convictions even though it was unpopular.

You do not have to be obnoxious to be bold and courageous. You can be respectful of the opinions of others while still holding firm to the path God has for you. You do not always have to explain your decisions. In the end, your loyalty to obey Christ should speak for itself. Remember that you alone will answer to God one day; be gracious when others disagree. Be kind and bold at the same time.

Keep your eyes on Jesus, and He will help you persevere under the misunderstandings of others.

The more the culture changes, the brighter your light should shine for the glory of God. Conforming to the world's pattern will not help them or you. You were placed on earth to be the light. Being different can be challenging, but it builds character.

How is God calling you to stand firm in obedience to Him?

Whatever Is Admirable

DAY 80

FREE FROM SELFISH GAIN

*Turn my heart toward your statutes and not
toward selfish gain.*

— PSALM 119:36

How can you know if you are working toward selfish gain? It is selfish if you have enough, but you take away from someone who does not. Just because it is available does not mean you should take advantage of the opportunity. This goes against human nature, but what does Christ call us to do? When we understand God will ensure we have all we need and more, we can be free from greed and grasping.

Fear tells us we must stockpile more than we need in case something unexpected happens. There is wisdom in reserving a little extra, but fear goes further. It never says you have enough.

Another form of selfish gain that stunts our growth is striving to be the center of attention. Have you known anyone who must ensure everyone sees them and knows they are in the room? This shows insecurity masking as confidence. They falsely believe that their worth is tied to being seen or admired. No one wants to admit this fault, but I encourage you to ask the Lord to search your heart. What lie might you believe that causes you to work overtime to present an image that is tiring to maintain? Christ sets us free from the constant need for approval from our peers. Because we belong to Him, our chief priority is to please Him, not ourselves.

Please understand the devil loves to deal in extremes. He either wants us to be self- absorbed or to suffer unnecessarily. He hates balance. Everyone can have their moment in the spotlight when earned, but a desperate drive for it is unhealthy and is prideful bondage. Think on these things and be free!

Whatever Is Right

༄

DAY 81
FOLLOW DIRECTIONS

*There is a way that appears to be right, but in the
end, it leads to death.*

— PROVERBS 14:12

What do Noah, Moses, the apostle John, and Jesus have in common? They all followed God's instructions. God gave Moses specific directions on how the
Tabernacle would be built and what materials to use. Noah received specific instructions on the ark's dimensions and followed every one of them. The apostle John, in the book of Revelation, heard God tell him what to write. At one point, he was about to write something, and God told him not to write it (Revelation 10:4).

John did whatever the Lord told him. Jesus told us He only did and said what the Father told Him (John 8:28).

Are you like this? Do you follow directions God gives? The temptation to improvise is real but detrimental. Our pride pulls us to do things our way and to lean on our understanding. We cheat ourselves of great blessings when we do not follow God's instructions (Proverbs 13:15).

What would have happened to the ark if Noah threw away God's blueprint and made it up as he went along? Would all the animals have fit? Remember how long it took for things to dry up? He and his family might have run out of food because he didn't build enough storage!

Moses had already escaped death once (Genesis 17:10-14), and he learned to do precisely what God said when He said it. He was not perfect, but He was faithful.

Has God's Spirit prompted you to do something, but you ignored it? We all have. If there is still time to obey, please do. Blessings await those who are obedient. Tune your heart to follow God's directions in every way today.

Whatever Is True

DAY 82

GOD WANTS YOU TO SUCCEED!

*Keep this Book of the Law always on your
lips; meditate on it day and night, so that
you may be careful to do everything written
in it. Then you will be prosperous and
successful.*

— JOSHUA 1:8

od wants you to succeed, and the Bible is your
success manual. He tells us how to succeed in
marriage, at work, in parenting, in handling conflict,
and in enforcing healthy boundaries. Why, then, do we neglect
the reading, meditating, and memorizing the Word? Why do we
allow social media to distract us? Why do we make excuses for
attending a small group and the corporate preaching of this
manual every week?

We know it is important and don't intend to slack in these
areas. We must practice intentionality if we are to grow, my
friend. Never forget you have a spiritual enemy who wants you

to fail. Your success threatens his agenda for your life and those of your children and grandchildren. We help him defeat us when we are lazy, distracted, and apathetic.

How can you ensure the success God planned for you? In addition to intentionality, key habits are essential. If you do anything often enough, you will notice whenever you don't do it. You will feel that something is off. If you are haphazard in your pursuits, you won't see a break in cadence. Add documentation to intentionality and key habits. Write down your goals and insights and track them regularly. You may use a calendar or an app on your phone to track progress. Pick a method you will stick with. Tracking is a form of meditation. You will see when you are trailing off course sooner and save time.

If you do your part, God will do His to help you succeed.

Whatever Is Noble

DAY 83
INVEST

And the things you have heard me say in the presence of many witnesses entrust to reliable people who will also be qualified to teach others.

— 1TIMOTHY 2:2

I f you know the gospel, you have a treasure to share with the world. The Good News is the single most powerful message that reaps eternal benefits.

What would happen if every person who received the gift of eternal life kept it to themselves? The next generation would be lost with nothing of eternal worth to pass on to their children, grandchildren, neighbors, and friends. Now, imagine that everyone who received Christ shared this good news with loved ones and friends.

What if those people then shared with their friends and family? Do you see the impact one life can make even long after they have passed away?

What about your life, my friend? How many people have you impacted by sharing the gospel? We have no power over what they do with it, but we have a God-given responsibility and fantastic privilege to let people know they have an eternal choice. How can they know if we don't tell them?

When we are privileged to lead someone to Christ, we get the joy of nurturing them in their newfound faith. Just as no sane person would leave a newborn lying in the street, no Christian should leave a new convert to fend for themselves. They need you to nurture them with the Word, connect them with a spiritual family, and train them in Christian living. Like parenting, it is a daunting task, I know, but the

Holy Spirit will do it through you. Your reward will be spiritual grandchildren and great-grands. Invest in what can never be stolen, corroded, or lost. Think on these

things.

Whatever Is Noble

DAY 84
NOT A BURDEN

*In fact, this is love for God: to keep his
commands. And his commands are
not burdensome.*

— 1 JOHN 5:3

In your weaker moments, do you secretly envy unbelievers who do whatever they want? Do you find keeping God's commands burdensome? What would make John say that God's commands are not a burden?

Think about what it means to care for someone you love who has limitations. They are self-conscious about needing your help, and you keep assuring them they are not a burden. You don't want them to feel they are an inconvenience in any way.

Why? Because you love them. Maybe they cared for you in your time of need, and you delight to return their kindness. Perhaps you have compassion because they have no one else to meet their needs, and you want to protect them from predators.

Caring for someone with limitations can be physically and mentally exhausting, but it does not mean it is burdensome. Love has a way of fueling our service, doesn't it?

Think of all God does for you, my friend. Meditate on the number of times He provides for you each day. Recall the state you were in when He found you and how He has changed you for the better. How can His commands be a burden in the face of so much grace? What could He ask that you that is too much? He has purchased blissful eternity and promised constant Companionship here on earth.

Who has given more to you than the Lord has?

Jesus said His yoke is easy and that His burden is light (Matthew 11:30). If you feel overwhelmed by Christian duty, ask the Lord to show you what you're missing. His commands are not burdensome. Think on these things.

Whatever is Admirable

DAY 85

BE UNSTOPPABLE

Let us not become weary in doing good, for at the
proper time we will reap a harvest if we do
not give up.

— GALATIANS 6:9

The only way to be unstoppable is not to stop. God loves to empower the weak and to champion the underdog. Our weaknesses are opportunities to show His glory.

The underdog has the odds stacked against her and nothing to lose. Again, underdogs provide prime scenarios for God to show up and perform miracles.

I love the determination of the apostle Paul. The man just wouldn't stop! If they put him in prison, he preached to the prisoners. If they dragged him into court, he proclaimed the gospel to the officials. If false teachers came in to confuse new believers, he corrected them in person or by letter. Nothing was going to stop him from fulfilling all God gave him to do.

What about you? Do you struggle with discouragement when obstacles keep getting in your way? Do you feel like giving up because people think your dream is unrealistic? Think of all the inventors throughout history who were laughed at until they proved their hecklers wrong.

Ordinary days take on fresh meaning when we see they are opportunities to build consistently. Keep building on your dream one day at a time, my friend. The hardest part may be not knowing when the waiting, praying, and preparing will end. Trust that God is at work behind the scenes. He is preparing you and other people so that the connection will be right when the time is right. It will all make sense. It will be worth it all. Think of these things and never quit.

Think On This

Satan changes the road signs to forbidden places, hides all the clocks, and turns up the music to drown out the voice of God.

Think on This

Even in walking

with God,

consistent baby
steps are more
productive than
occasional,

unsustainable leaps

of faith.

Whatever Is Worthy of Praise

∽∽∽

DAY 86
SMALL BUT MIGHTY

Who dares despise the day of small things?

— ZECHARIAH 4:10

We humans are obsessed with the size of things: big houses, big ministries, and big money. We are drawn to big social media followings and people who impact lives on a large scale. Nothing is wrong with those things, but we must not despise the value of small things. The poor would rather you give a small amount than withhold it, waiting for a big check you may never get to write. A kind word to a discouraged soul makes a huge impact. A simple phone call to a depressed friend can save a life and all the lives that person will touch.

Jesus said if anyone gives a cup of cold water in His name, he will reap a reward. (Matthew 10:42). God is not impressed by big things because He is bigger than all of them. His heart and hand move at faith the size of a mustard seed.

I've heard charity workers apologize for the size of their

gifts, wishing they could give more. Please don't underestimate what God can do with your small gift when it is your best offer. Small gifts given regularly over time are how most ministries survive. Ignore the voice of the enemy who mocks the size of your donation. He desires to shame you into not giving at all. Only heaven will reveal how far your contribution stretched and how many received blessings through what you gave.

We will all be surprised when the Father dispenses rewards on that great Day.

Many small gifts will receive big rewards, and some big gifts will yield no reward because of shallow motives. Give with a big heart, and do not despise small offerings given or received.

Whatever Is Noble

DAY 87

WAITING ON GOD

*Wait for the Lord; be strong and take heart and
wait for the Lord.*

— PSALM 27:14

Waiting is hard. It's also a necessary part of life. Because you cannot control time, people, or circumstances, waiting gives you the humility to yield to the One Who controls all three.

Waiting on God is different from waiting on people because God has full access to everything involved in your situation. You will never introduce new data to Him to speed Him up in your favor. He knows how long you've been waiting and how deep your longing is. He knows how tired you are of waiting, and He knows about the moments you give up in frustration, even if only temporarily. And yet, He still has you waiting. (Sigh)

It comes down to trust. Trust is a choice. Just like griping, rushing ahead, or spiritual eye-rolling, trusting God is a choice. If you are sure of His love for you—a love that knows and wants what's best for you— then waiting is a form of loving Him back.

What does waiting well look like in your life?

One more thing: I've discovered that the season of waiting is rich with opportunities to grow in patience, self-discovery, and, best of all, intimacy with

God. He offers His lap to sit on in His waiting room. His voice can be clearer in the quiet (now that the whining has stopped) of His waiting room. This waiting time might even enhance your enjoyment of whatever you are waiting for when it finally arrives. I suspect God also wants us to realize that a relationship with Him is better than whatever we are waiting for.

Let's do a better job at waiting on God in the right way.

Whatever Is Noble

HANDLING INSULTS NOBLY

Do not repay evil with evil or insult with insult. On the contrary, repay evil with blessing, because to this you were called so that you may inherit a blessing.

— 1 PETER 3:9

When someone insults you, the last thing you want to do is to bless them, but that is what Christ calls you to do, my friend. The apostle Peter wrote to followers of Christ who were persecuted for their faith. He instructed them to keep a tender heart and a humble attitude (1 Peter 3:8). He charged them not to take revenge but to bless their persecutors. Is this counterintuitive, or what? Everything in us wants to beat our insulters, not bless them.

Be encouraged, my friend. God never gives you an impossible task without making it possible by His Spirit. You can do all things through Christ, Who gives you strength, including controlling your "get even" muscle. You have the mind of

Christ, which means you can think with the thoughts of Christ toward your enemies. You can love them with the same love God showed you when you were

His enemy. It's supernatural, and you have the key to heaven's storehouse of strength for the task. Pray that your love for God will be stronger than your dislike for your enemy. You are not on trial when someone insults you; your faith is. God wants to use you to show the people around you what it looks like to follow Christ in hard times. It is the assignment of every believer.

The reward will be worth the difficulty, my friend. The Spirit told Peter to write that you will receive a blessing when you obey God in this way. The smile of God is sweeter than any revenge.

Whatever Is Pure

DAY 89
YOUR THIRD EYE

*He faced the fact that his body was as good as
dead...and that Sarah's womb was also dead.
Yet he did not waver through unbelief
regarding the promise of God... being fully
persuaded that God had power to do what he
had promised.*

— ROMANS 4:19-21

My heartbeat speeds up every time I read the passage above.

I have noticed that overcomers use their two natural eyes to look at bare-naked facts. They don't dabble in denial and tell themselves they don't see what is staring back at them. But while they view the facts with their natural eyes, they also have a third eye, the eye of faith.

Do you have three eyes?

People call us crazy, pie-in-the-sky Pollyannas because of our third eye, but we are more realistic than pessimists. We know once God makes a promise, it is as real as if it already happened. We remember that God sees the past, present, and future simultaneously and makes promises in view of all three. He already sees the promise fulfilled. Our third eye sees it, too.

What has God promised that you are tempted to doubt? If your third eye is getting blurry, you may be looking too long at the circumstance and not enough at the One

Who is greater than your circumstances.

Verse 20 of today's passage says Abraham was strengthened in his faith. Where did his faith find its strength? In the power of God! You don't have to muster up faith if it's faith in God because His promises are backed up by who He is and what He can do!

Today, renew your strength by keeping your natural eyes open and your third eye focused on the power of God.

Whatever Is Lovely

~~~

DAY 90

THE PERKS OF WEAKNESS

*My grace is sufficient for you, for my power is
made perfect in weakness.*

— 2 CORINTHIANS 12:9

Have you noticed that when God calls someone in the Bible to do something, they point out weaknesses that disqualify them from the task? Do you tend to do that? I think it is human nature to ask God, *"Who, me?"*

I remember the dental van coming to my public elementary school once a year when I was a child. They would always show a film about proper dental care and send us home with a new toothbrush and some pink tablets that dissolved in our mouths. The pills were the most fun part because after brushing, we sucked on the tablets to see where we missed brushing. The goal was to have no pink showing, but as kids, we took delight in seeing how pink our teeth and tongue turned. Could it be that when your heavenly Daddy decides how He wants to be glorified in your life, He looks for the pink spots where your weakness is most pronounced? You see your pink spots as reasons God should choose someone else, but God sees those same flaws as places to apply His grace and bring glory to Himself. He applies His power in those places, and it becomes obvious He is the One doing great things through you.

The apostle Paul declared that because Christ's power would rest on him, he would rather boast about his weakness. I know it's kind of uncomfortable to think of your weakness in this way. You'd rather it was not there. But since it is a part of your beautiful yet imperfect self, why not let God re-purpose it?

Appendix

Also by Dr. Georgia Pointer

A Christians Woman's
Guide to
Overcoming
Messy

EMOTIONS

———

BY DR. GEORGIA POINTER

An Encouragem8ent Outpost Book